STUDIES IN HEBREW CULTURE

*

THE SYNAGOGUE

STUDIES IN HEBREW CULTURE

Series compiled by
JESUS PELAEZ

Books published:

1. Jesús Peláez del Rosal (ed.), *The Jews in Córdoba (X-XII Centuries)*.
2. Jesús Peláez del Rosal, *The Synagogue*.

In preparation:

Tamar Alexander and Elena Romero: *Once upon a time... Maimonides. An anthology of traditional Hebrew tales*.
Angeles Navarro: *Spanish Hebrew Literature (X-XIII centuries). A Panorama*.

JESÚS PELÁEZ DEL ROSAL

THE SYNAGOGUE

EDICIONES EL ALMENDRO
CORDOBA - MADRID

First Published by Ediciones El Almendro, Córdoba 1988,
with the title: *La Sinagoga.*

Translated into English by PATRICIA A. SNEESBY

Front cover:

Women's gallery. Southern wall, Córdoba synagogue
(photo by Huedo).

Back cover:

Foundation inscription. Eastern wall, Córdoba synagogue
(photo by Huedo).

EDICIONES EL ALMENDRO DE CORDOBA, S. L.

El Almendro, 10   Donoso Cortés, 22, 2.º dcha.
Telephone No. (957) 27 46 92   Telephone No. (91) 593 26 94
14006 CÓRDOBA   28015 MADRID

ISBN: 84-86077-79-6
Depósito legal: M. 22.010-1990

Printed in Spain.

ARTES GRÁFICAS BENZAL, S. A. Virtudes, 7. 28010 MADRID

For Antonio and Obdulia, grandparents,
for Salvador and Antonia, parents,
and for Antonio, son,
custodians of the Córdoba synagogue

CONTENTS

PART I:
THE SYNAGOGUE

9

PREFACE

When I began to write this book my intention was to provide a complete guide to the Córdoba synagogue, for, inexplicable as it may seem, no complete guide to this monument exists at all. But as I studied this historical synagogue, unique in Andalusia and one of the only three mediaeval synagogues that still survive in Spain, I began to realize that a description is of little use if the reader has not first of all seen the reasons behind its existence, its history and its functions, for it takes second place in importance among Jewish institutions perhaps only to the Jerusalem temple itself. For many centuries the life of the Jewish people has revolved around the synagogue, so much so that we may say that the synagogue has been its heart, centre or axis and this is still true today.

And so this book, which set out as a guide to the synagogue in Córdoba, in its first part presents a study of the synagogue as an institution and in the second the first complete guide to the Córdoba synagogue. Thus it will be of use not only to those who desire an introduction into the understanding of the synagogue institution, but also to those who wish, either in situ or from a distance, to approach the history of the Córdoba synagogue and its architectural, artistic and epigraphical values.

The Synagogue as an Institution (first part of this book, chapters I-VIII) has been dealt with in magnificent works in other languages, but in Spanish (the language this study was originally written in) there was no complete work available to the general public: so this book may serve as reference for those who wish to study the institution from different points of view.

15

On the Córdoba synagogue *the excellent works referred to in the Bibliography are either prior to 1950 or intended for specialized readers, versed in the subject, and with a knowledge of Hebrew, like the magnificent study of Córdoba by Father Francisco Cantera Burgos* Sinagogas españolas *(C.S.I.C., Madrid 1955, reprinted in offset in 1983, pages 3-32) which I consider unsurpassable.*

So the second part of this book is dedicated to the synagogue in Córdoba. After a brief description of mediaeval synagogues, with special mention of the Santa María la Blanca and the Tránsito in Toledo (chap. VIII), a panorama is presented of the Jews' situation in Córdoba in the XIII-XV centuries (chap. IX), the history of the Córdoba synagogue is related with its successive restorations and modifications (chap. X) and the monument is explained from architectural, artistic and epigraphical points of view (chap. XI).

Chapter XI, «Two visits to the Córdoba synagogue», presents a double vision of the monument: one, in detail, covers all the existing information enriched with new evidence; the other is a brief vision for those who wish to cover just the essential points.

Chapters X and XI, dedicated to the Córdoba synagogue, centre on the study of the synagogue itself (entrance and prayer hall) and on the custodian's dwelling, leaving the study of adjacent houses for another occasion. As far as the latter are concerned, an urgent architectural study needs to be carried out together with archaeological research to identify their ancient structures, as far as is possible, and to ascertain whether they origianlly formed part of the synagogue complex. It would also be useful to carry out an archaeological survey of the site next to the synagogue's north wall, as well as an inspection of the bottom of the wells in adjacent houses in order to discover, from pottery found in them, the period in which they were in use.

Our wish is that this contribute to an awareness, both within and without Córdoba, of the enormous importance of this monument of Spanish Mediaeval Judaism — second only in visiting public to the Mosque — and to rescue it from the forsaken state it has been in for such a long time, placing it on a par with its two contemporaries: the Santa María la Blanca and the Tránsito synagogues in Toledo.

As a book destined for an ample range of readers, footnotes have been avoided, including them in the main body of the text when convenient. Authors and works (articles and books) have been quoted

16

in abbreviated form. The reader may consult the Bibliographical Selection (page 175) for the key to abbreviations used to refer to authors who appear relatively frequently. For the numerous abbreviations for books of the Bible, Mishna tractates, Talmud and works by Philo and Josephus Flavius, see pages 19-21.

As several technical terms have had to be used we have included a Glossary with a brief aclaration of the most important, see pages 179-185.

I can only end by expressing my gratitude to all who have contributed, one way or another, to the appearance of this book. First of all to Lucía Rubiano who helped me collect all the bibliography for the second part; to fellow professors and readers of Arab Language and Literature, Ana Labarta and Carmen Barceló, who contributed with the description of the Mudéjar plasters and the reading and translation of the Arab inscriptions on the west and east walls; to the director of C.S.I.C. publications for his permission to reproduce various illustrations from Francisco Cantera's book already mentioned; to J. M. Escobar Camacho also for his permission to reproduce a plan from his as yet unpublished work The City of Córdoba in the Lower Middle Ages; *to Joaquín Serrano, architect, for allowing us to reproduce several plans of the Synagogue and the Custodian's dwelling; to the Cultural Delegation of the Andalusian Government, Córdoba, for having facilitated the file on the Synagogue for consultation and for having contributed the photographs taken under commission by Mr. Huedo by the said Delegation for other purposes; to Mr. Huedo who generously permitted their publication and to Francisco González, photographer for the* Diario Córdoba *newspaper, unconditional collaborator on other books in the series as well as the present one.*

Jesús Peláez del Rosal

ABBREVIATIONS

BOOKS OF THE BIBLE

Gn	Genesis	Prv	Proverbs
Ex	Exodus	Eccl	Ecclesiastes (Qoheleth)
Lv	Leviticus	Ct	Canticle of Canticles
Nm	Numbers	Wis	Wisdom
Dt	Deuteronomy	Sir	Sirach (Ecclesiasticus)
Jos	Joshua	Is	Isaiah
Jgs	Judges	Jer	Jeremiah
Ru	Ruth	Lam	Lamentations
1 Sm	1 Samuel	Bar	Baruch
2 Sm	2 Samuel	Ez	Ezekiel
1 Kgs	1 Kings	Dn	Daniel
2 Kgs	2 Kings	Hos	Hosea
1 Chr	1 Chronicles	Jl	Joel
2 Chr	2 Chronicles	Am	Amos
Ezr	Ezra	Obd	Obadiah
Neh	Nehemiah	Jon	Jonah
Tb	Tobit	Mi	Micah
Jdt	Judith	Na	Nahum
Est	Esther	Hab	Habbakkuk
1 Mc	1 Maccabees	Zeph	Zephaniah
2 Mc	2 Maccabees	Hag	Haggai
Jb	Job	Zech	Zechariah
Ps	Psalms	Mal	Malachi

Mt	Matthew	1 Tm	1 Timothy
Mk	Mark	2 Tm	2 Timothy
Lk	Luke	Tit	Titus
Jn	John	Phlm	Philemon
Acts	Acts of the Apostles	Heb	Hebrews
Rom	Romans	Jas	James
1 Cor	1 Corinthians	1 Pt	1 Peter
2 Cor	2 Corinthians	2 Pt	2 Peter
Gal	Galatians	1 Jn	1 John
Eph	Ephesians	2 Jn	2 John
Phil	Philippians	3 Jn	3 John
Col	Colossians	Jude	Jude
1 Thess	1 Thessalonians	Rev	Apocalypse
2 Thess	2 Thessalonians		

RABBINIC WRITINGS (TRACTATES OF THE MISHNA)

Ab	'Aḅot	Me'i	Mě'ilah
Arak	'Ăraḵin	Men	Měnaḥot
A.Z.	'Ăbodah Zarah	Mid	Middot
Bek	Běḵorot	Miq	Miqwaot
Ber	Běraḵot	M.Q.	Mo'ed Qatan
Bez	Beṣah	M.Š.	Ma'aśer šeni
B.B.	Baba' Batra'	Naz	Nazir
Bik	Bikkurim	Ned	Nědarim
B.M.	Baba' Meṣia'	Neg	Něga'im
B.Q.	Baḅa' Qamma'	Nid	Niddah
Dem	Děmay	Ohol	Oholot
Ed	'Eduyyot	Orl	'Orlah
Erub	'Eruḅin	Par	Parah
Git	Gittin	Pe'a	Peah
Hag	Ḥagigah	Pes	Pěsaḥim
Hall	Ḥallah	Qin	Qinnin
Hor	Horayot	R.H.	Roš Hašanah
Hull	Ḥullin	Šab	Šabbat
Kel	Kelim	Sanh	Sanhedrin
Ker	Kěritot	Šebi	Sebi'it
Ket	Kětuḅot	Šeb	Sěbu'ot
Kid	Kiddušim	Šek	Šěkalim
Kil	Kil'ayim	Sot	Sotah
Ma'as	Ma'aśrot	Sukk	Sukkah
Makk	Makkot	Ta'an	Ta'anit
Makš	Makširim	Tam	Tamid
Meg	Měgillah	Teb	Těḅul yom

Tem	Těmurah	Yeb	Yěbamot
Ter	Těrumot	Yom	Yoma'
Ṭoḥ	Ṭŏḥorot	Zab	Zaḅim
Ukṣ	Ukṣim	Zeb	Zěḅahim
Yad	Yadadayim	Zer	Zěra'im

Mishna passages are referred to by chapter and section: e.g. Ber 4,1. The abbreviations used follow the initial letters of the individuals tractates.

OTHER ABBREVIATIONS

BT	Babilonian Talmud	S. 'Ar	Šulhan 'Aruk
PT	Palestinian Talmud	Tos	Tosefta'
Pesik	Pesikta	Tanh	Tanhuma'
R	Rabbah		

WORKS OF PHILO

De Abr.	De Abrahamo	De Spec. Leg.	De specialibus legibus
Flacc.	In Flaccum	De Vita Cont.	De vita contemplativa si-
De Leg.	De Legatione ad Gaium		ve supplicum virtutibus
De Opif.	De opificio mundi	De Vita Mos.	De vita Mosis

WORKS OF FLAVIUS JOSEPHUS

Ant.	Antiquitates
Apion.	Contra Apionem
Bell.	De bello Iudaico

GENERAL ABBREVIATIONS

Aram	aramaic	col.	column
A.D.	Anno Domini	gr.	greek
b.	bar/ben (Aram./Heb.)	heb.	hebreo
	son of	i.e.	i.d. (Làt.), that is
B.C.	before Christ	NT	New Testament
c.	circa (Lat.) about, aproxi-	OT	Old Testament
	mately	p., pp.	page, pages
cent.	century	R.	Rabbi
Cf.	confer (compare)	vol.	volume
ch(s).	chapter(s)	vs., vss.	verse, verses

PART I
THE SYNAGOGUE

CHAPTER I

THE ORIGINS OF THE SYNAGOGUE

1. NAMES FOR THE SYNAGOGUE

Synagôgê

The word synagogue comes from the Greek *synagôgê*, derived from the verb *synagô* which means «to congregate, to meet». Hence synagogue is the meeting or meeting-place of the Jews.

In Hebrew synagogue is called *kĕneset* or *bet ha-kĕneset* (meeting or meeting-house); in Aramaean *kĕništa'*, or *be(t) kĕništa'*.

In the LXX version or Greek Bible, *synagôgê* is frequently used to translate the Hebrew term *'edah* (congregation) and sometimes *kahal* (assembly).

In Aramaean versions of the Bible, *'edah* is always translated as *kĕništa'* (in Syrian *kĕnušta'*) which, like *synagôgê*, means meeting. This term, according to some researchers, very soon took on the specific meaning of meeting for prayer and instruction; this is the meaning in Neh 8-9, when reference is later made to the meeting for public reading of the law with the expression *kĕneset ha-gĕdolah* (the great synagogue).

In the New Testament and in Jewish authors like Philo and Flavius Josephus, *synagôgê* often means place of worship and meeting of the Jews, as we shall see further on. Tannaitic literature uses the expression *bet ha-kĕneset* when referring to the meeting-place, whilst *kĕneset* on its own is a meeting with no reference to a specific place.

Proseukhê

Another word used to indicate the Jews' meeting-place is *proseukhê* (prayer), a metonymic use of the word in the sense of place

25

of prayer, corresponding to the Hebrew expression *bet-tĕfillah* (house of prayer) in Is 56:7. The denomination *Proseukhê* can be traced as far back as the beginning of the first century from an inscription found in the synagogue at Delos. It appears mainly in Philo *(Flacc.* 6,14; *De Leg.* 20,43,46), Flavius Josephus (De Vita Mos. 54) and once in the New Testament (Acts 16:13).

Some have taken *proseukhê* as a reference to a certain type of synagogue, a sort of small chapel outside the city by a river, or prayer meeting in open spaces. For others, *proseukhê* is the term used by Hellenistic Jews in Egypt and standard in Greece, Asia Minor and Rome, whilst *synagôgê* is of Palestinian origin.

Philo (De Vita Mos. 2,39 [216]) calls the synagogues *proseukhtêria.*

Other denominations

As well as *synagôgê* and *proseukhê,* to be found in literary and epigraphic sources to name the synagogue as the Jews' meeting place, it is also referred to by other Greek names, which come exclusively from epigraphical material and have a Hebrew or Aramaean equivalent, related to words and expressions which in the Hebrew Bible refer to places of worship. They are:

— *topos* (place); sometimes *hagios topos* (holy place); see Isaac's sacrifice, Gn 22:3-4,9,14; Jacob's dream, Gn 28:11,16-17 and the burning bush, Ex 3:5. These three scenes, each referring to a particular place (gr. *topos),* occupy a prominent place in the decoration of the Synagogue at Dura Europos in Babylonia, which shows that the Jews related them closely to the synagogue as a place of worship and communion with God.

— *oikos* (house, temple) translates the Hebrew expression *habayit* which designates the temple in Jerusalem and appears on two inscriptions in the synagogue at Dura Europos. (Viz. Solomon's prayer in 1 Kings 8:22ff, where *bayit* [temple] appears in relation to prayers and worship.)

— *sabbateion,* mentioned in an edict of Emperor Augustus (Jos., *Ant.* 16,6,2) originates from the fact that synagogue worship took place on the Sabbath. This name appears neither in Hebrew nor Aramaean but it does in late Syrian.

— *didaskaleion,* place of teaching where the forefathers' philosophy is cultivated together with all kinds of teaching of virtues. In Philo (De Vita Mos. 2,39 [216]). In the Gospels the principal activity accorded to the synagogues is that of teaching *(didaskein;* cf. Mt 4:23; Mk 1:21; 6:2; Lk 4:15,31; 6:6; 13:10; Jn 6:59; 18:20).

2. THE SYNAGOGUE IN BIBLICAL TEXTS

The synagogue and the temple are the two most important institutions in Judaism. However, whilst for the historical origins of the temple we have an ample biblical narration, the origins of the synagogue are very obscure.

Ezekiel

For some, the earliest reference to the synagogue is to be found in the book of the prophet Ezekiel. Different researchers have suggested that the repeated mention to the assemblies of the elders before Ezekiel (8:1; 14:1; 20:1) may refer to the beginnings of the synagogue as an institution. The reference to the «little sanctuary» in Ez 11:16, identified by the Talmud (BT Meg 29a) as the synagogue, is clearer: *Therefore say, Thus saith the Lord God; Although I have cast them far off among the heathen, and although I have scattered them among the countries, yet will I be to them as a little sanctuary in the countries where they shall come.* The expression «little sanctuary» could perhaps mean, within the context of the Babylonian exile, the role of the synagogue for lack of a temple.

When quoting the Mishna, the Babylonian Talmud and the Palestinian Talmud, we shall use the following:

Mishna: M followed by the abbreviated title of the tractate, chapter and page numbers. For example: «M Ta'an» 4,2 refers to *Mishna,* «Ta'anit» tractate, chapter 4, page 2.

Babylonian Talmud: BT, followed by the abbreviated title of the tractate, number and letter. For example: «BT Ber 33a» refers to the «Babylonian Talmud», «Běrakot» tractate, number «33», letter «a».

Palestinian or Jerosolimitan Talmud: PT, followed by abbreviated title of the tractate, number and letter. For example: «PT, Meg 75c» refs to the «Palestinian Talmud», «Megillah» tractate, number «75», letter «c».

The list of abbreviations for the books of the Bible, the Targums, Rabbinic literature, tractates from the Mishna and Talmud (Babilonian and Palestinian), as well as works by Philo and Josephus Flavius will be found on pages 19 to 21.

«Technical Terms» used throughout the book can be consulted in the Glossary on pages 179 to 185.

Authors' works referred to throughout this book are quoted in abbreviated form. Cf. Bibliography on pages 175-177.

Psalm 74

Other authors appear to see in Psalm 74 a veiled allusion to the synagogue. Verse 8 of this Psalm reads: «They said in their hearts, Let us destroy them together; They have burned up all the synagogues of God in the land» (Ps 74:8).

«Assemblies of God» (heb. *mo'ăde-'el)* is a frequent synonym for *kahal* (meeting, congregation). The Greek version of the LXX, however, does not use the term *synagôgê* to translate this expression, but *heortê,* which means solemnity, feast day, feast time. Aramaean versions of the Bible translate *'edah* as *kĕništa',* giving *kĕneset,* but this word, like *synagôgê,* means «meeting» in the Old Testament and does not refer to any particular building or meeting place.

Moreover, even if the expression *mo'ăde-'el* (synagogues of God) were to indicate the meeting places where the assemblies were held, this does not solve the problem of the synagogue's origins, as we do not know exactly when Psalm 74 was composed, varying from those who date it in the times of the fall of Jerusalem in 586 B.C., an opinion that has predominated in recent years, to others who relate it to the situation produced by the profanation of the temple in times of Antiochus Epiphanes (168 B.C.), an opinion that has been held for almost two centuries. According to these two ways of thinking, the dating of the synagogue would run parallel to that of the Psalm.

Yet others have seen in the expression *bet ha-'am* in Jer 39:8 (the houses of the people burned by the Chaldeans on taking Jerusalem in 586 B.C.) a kind of embrionic synagogue, of secular origin, buildings for public meetings of a civil character that would gradually become synagogues. Cf. Leopold Löw *(Der Synagogale Ritus).*

Maccabees

Nor are we sure of the existence of synagogues in Maccabees' time — even though some have stated that the reference to Mizpeh in 1 Mc 3:46ff as a place of prayer (in Greek *topos proseukhês)* does not indicate a sanctuary, but a synagogue. At all events, even if the reference here is not to a synagogue, one thing is quite clear: in 1 Mc. 3:48 reference is made to the public reading of a Torah volume and in 4:24 to the singing of hymns: «And they returned home, and sang a song of thanksgiving, and gave praise unto heaven; because his mercy is good, because his mercy endureth for ever». Public reading and hymn singing form integral parts of the synagogue liturgy from the very beginning.

Except for these quotations, in which some see veiled allusions to synagogues as buildings or meeting places of the Jews, the Old Testament or Jewish Bible makes no mention of a synagogue building.

New Testament, Flavius Josephus and Philo

At the beginning of our time, however, both New Testament and Jewish authors — Flavius Josephus and Philo — use ever more frequently the term *synagôgê* in their writings in the sense of the Jews' place or house of worship, meeting and study. Another term used quite commonly to indicate the Jews' public place of worship is *proseukhê,* as has already been indicated, a Greek word meaning «worship» used in the sense of «place of worship».

3. THE ORIGINS OF THE SYNAGOGUE INSTITUTION

From the beginnings of the Hebrew people

Various passages from Targum Pseudo-Jonathan to Exodus (18:20) as well as Midrash (Yal Ex 408), take the synagogues' existence for granted almost from the beginnings of the Hebrew people. In the book of the Acts of the Apostles (15:21), James considers the synagogue as a very ancient institution: «For Moses of old time hath in every city them that preach him, being read in the synagogues every sabbath day». Philo (De Vita Mos. 3,17) and Flavius Josephus (Ap. 2,17,75) make it quite clear that the synagogue institution goes back to Moses. In the XVII century, H. Grotius defends this same point of view.

From the era of the First Temple (prior to 638 B.C.)

Among recent authors, I. Levy *(The Synagogue)* holds that the synagogue as an institution goes back to the times of the First Temple (prior to 638 B.C.). J. Weingreen *(The Origin)* makes the same statement, based on diverse Bible passages. According to the latter, sacrifices were accompanied by prayers in the local sanctuaries; so, when Joshua forbade sacrificial rites in these sanctuaries (4 Kgs 22 and 23), worship without sacrifices, typical of the synagogue, continued there. Indeed, in Psalm 116:17 and Isaiah 1:11-15 the sacrifices are accompanied by prayers; in Shiloh, Hannah's prayer is not followed by sacrifices (1 Sm 1:10ff) and in 4 Kgs 22-23, during the dedication of the temple, nor is Solomon's prayer accompanied by any sacrifice. These are the texts used by I. Levy as a basis to state that the synagogue's origins are to be found in the period of the first temple, and that the existence of worship without sacrifices, similar to that typical of the synagogue, dates back to this time.

After Josiah and before the Exile (621-587 B.C.)

Another very extended opinion is the one maintained by scholars that the synagogue as an institution existed before the Exile (587 B.C.), appearing as a consequence of Josiah's reform.

Josiah, King of Judah, reigned from 638 to 608 B.C. His reign was characterized by a series of political-religious measures, the most outstanding of which are the centralization of Yahweh's worship around the temple at Jerusalem and the abolition of worship to other gods like Baal, Ashtoreth and others. During his reign the temple at Jerusalem was repaired and as from that moment became the only legitimate place of worship, and all the priests in Judah «from Geba to Beer-sheba» were gathered here. He demolished all the sanctuaries consecrated to Yahweh outside Jerusalem, called «high places or altars» (2 Kgs 23:5,8-9) among which was the famous Beth-El sanctuary (2 Kgs 23:15).

In 621 B.C., when repairs were carried out on the temple at Jerusalem, a book of the Law was found, containing the nucleus of the book of Deuteronomy, undoubtedly the source of inspiration for Josiah's reform.

So this was how believers in the country and villages, on being deprived of sanctuaries and sacrificial rites with the centralization of cult in Jerusalem, adopted the custom of meeting together on certain days in their respective homes in order to worship without sacrificial service. Only on important feasts would they congregate in the temple at Jerusalem. And so the synagogue would become a sort of substitute for the temple, but with no animal offerings.

During the Babylonian exile (587-537 B.C.)

In the seventeenth century, however, Carolus Sigonius *(De republica),* expert on Greek and Roman political institutions, stated that the synagogue's origin could not be so ancient. In his opinion, it seems rather that the synagogue goes back as far as the Babylonian captivity (587 B.C.), as in the books of Judges and Kings no reference to it is to be found. In Sigonius' opinion, the synagogue began when the people, exiled and without a temple in Babylonia, felt the need to continue meeting to celebrate, pray, study and remember their sacred traditions.

The exile, a national desaster, put Israel's faith to a sore trial, and even provoked many to apostasy. For one sector of the exiles, the temple's destruction and the disappearance of worship seemed obvious proof that the Babylonian gods were mightier than the God of Israel; another sector, prepared by the preachings of Jeremiah and, above all, Ezekiel, who lived in exile along with them, discovered a meaning in what they were undergoing: God had not abandoned His people, He wanted to purify them putting them to the test of exile. Suspended all official worship and far away from the Jerusalem temple, it was still possible to meditate on past and present events and to pray to the Lord. This group of faithful began to meet wherever they could to help each other revive their faith; on the beach, by a river or by Babylon's canals, near the city where the exiles lived, as the psalm so delightfully sings: «By the rivers of Babylon, there we sat down, yea, we wept, when we remembered Zion. We hanged our harps upon the willows in the midst thereof...» (Ps 137:1-2).

Later, those among the exiled Jews who never returned to Palestine, remaining in Babylon or scattering throughout the world, retained this custom of meeting together to keep their faith firm in the Lord Yahweh and reaffirm their conscience of being the chosen people.

This movement became so generalized that in the first century of our era, as we shall see further on, every Jewish community had its synagogue; populous cities like Jerusalem, Rome, Alexandria or Antioch had several. It seems that the synagogues in the same city displayed special emblems, depending on the acceptance or not of the interpretation that in Sephoris existed a «vine synagogue» and in Rome an «olive synagogue».

After the Exile, in Ezra's time (515 B.C.)

On the other hand, in the nineteenth century C.V.Vitringa *(De Synagoga)* maintained that the ideal place for the birth of the synagogue as a universally accepted institution was not during the exile, but that it originated on the exiles' return to Palestine, during the Persian period, in times of Ezra and his successors, the scribes (515 B.C.).

These theories have been adopted by researchers like Krochmal, Zunz, Graetz, Wellhausen and Schürer who consider that although the synagogue originated in Babylonia during the exile as a substitute for temple worship, its consolidation as an institution came about on the exiles' return to Palestine, as a result of Ezra's efforts. Indeed the Babylonian Talmud (Ber 33a) attributes the formulation of the most ancient prayers (the *'Amidah, Kiddŭs* and *Habdalah*), which are typical forms of synagogue prayer, to Ezra and his successors, the men of the Great Synagogue.

Ezra (God is help), was a priest to the Jews in Babylon, «expert advocate of the Law given by the Lord, God of Israel, by means of Moses» (Ezr 7:1-5) and in all probability, counsellor for Jewish affairs to the Persian government. He was sent from Persia to Jerusalem to reorganize the situation of the post-exile Jewish community, according to Jewish Law. Ezra went up to Jerusalem together with about 1,500 Jews, who were joined in Casiphia (unidentifiable today) by 238 Levites and temple servants. Once there, in a great assembly, he proclaimed the law to which the Jews submitted themselves by a renewal of the covenant (Neh 8-10); later he denounced the many mixed marriages (Ezr 9ff); then it seems he was called back to Persia. The book of Ezra transcribes the copy of the letter that the king Artexerxes gave unto Ezra (Ezr 7:13ff).

With Ezra a new intellectual and religious class appeared in the history of the Jews: the scribe or expert in the Law. This office could very well have emerged and developed in exile, when sacrificial cult was lacking, so priests only conserved the function of official interpreters of the Law. A century later, when the prophets' class came to an end, the expert in law would see his authority increase. The Law was a literary corpus, which the scribes helped to select, determine, preserve and transmit. This is where the legend could have come from attributing the creation of the first canon of Hebrew scripture to Ezra.

So there is insufficient clear information to be able to state exactly when the synagogues began to exist as buildings or meeting places in Palestine or in the diaspore. To all events, it is to be supposed that they came about little by little.

From the moment worship was centralized, with King Josiah's reform (621 B.C.) the need was felt to seek places for prayer without sacrificial worship outside Jerusalem; taking into account the importance of the Torah, it would be read and explained to the Jews in places which, as time passed, would come to be called synagogues.

4. WRITTEN EVIDENCE ON SYNAGOGUES FROM THE FIRST CENTURIES OF OUR ERA

The New Testament

At the beginning of our era, the texts from the New Testament provide sufficient documentation on the existence of synagogues in all the land of Israel, where Jesus went to teach on the Sabbath as was His custom. Among them particular mention is made of two in Galilee: the one at Nazareth (Mk 6:2; Mt 13:54; Lk 4:16) and at Capernaum (Mk 1:21; Lk 4:33; 7:5; Jn 6:59). The Talmud adds another, the Alexandrians' synagogue in Jerusalem (Tos Meg 3,6; PT Meg 73d) and the Tharsis synagogue (BT Meg 26a), although it seems that both quotations refer to the same synagogue.

No archaeological remains have been found of the synagogues at Nazareth and Capernaum referred to in the Gospels. The Nazareth synagogue which can be visited today is nothing but an ancient building which, tradition has it, occupies the place of the synagogue of Jesus' times, but there is no archaeological evidence to support this tradition. The remains of the Capernaum synagogue go back no further than the third century of our era.

In the book of the Acts of the Apostles it is said that Paul preached in the synagogues in Damascus (Acts 9:2,20) and the cities he visited in Asia Minor are named (Salamis: 13:5; Antioch in Pisidia: 13:14; Thessalonica: 17:1; Corinth: 18:4,7; Ephesus: 18:19,26 and 19:8). Some of these cities, like Salamis in Cyprus, had more than one synagogue, no mention being made of exactly how many. This book refers to other synagogues too: that of the Libertines (6:9), the one at Iconium (14:1), Beroea (17:10) and

Athens (17:17). The apostles made them their point of departure for preaching and, if it had not been for them, the initial spreading of Christianity would have been extremely difficult. The early Christians, in order perhaps to distinguish themselves from the Jews, adopted the term *ekklêsia* instead of *synagôgê* to refer to their meetings.

The writings of the rabbis

The rabbis' writings show extensive evidence of the existence of synagogues, not only in Israel but also throughout the Diaspora in Asia (Turkey) and Europe.

The Mishna supplies many details of synagogue service on Mount Zion in *Yom Kippur* (Day of Atonement): «the synagogue *hazzan* takes the book of the Torah and hands it to the head of the synagogue who passes it to the prefect who passes it to the High Priest who takes it and, standing, reads...» (Sot 7,7). Likewise, in the description of the *Sukkot* feast (Feast of Tabernacles), Joshua ben Hananiah describes how the day was spent attending sacrifices in the temple and prayer in the synagogue (BT Sukk 53a)... Also, service duties in the temple and in the synagogue were arranged so that while the *mišmar* or guard duty of the priests, levites and Israelite representatives was doing its weekly turn in the temple, the rest of the members of the *ma'ămad* (synagogue guard duty), who belonged to the same class and had not been able to accompany them to Jerusalem, met together in their respective synagogues to pray and fast (M Ta'an 4,2). This reference from the Mishna sets out the fasting days in that week on duty as well as the readings and number of readers at the synagogue service each day.

The Babylonian Talmud describes a great synagogue where the members of different groups met, a synagogue so large that the chanter's voice could not be heard, it being necessary to wave flags to tell the congregation when to respond (Sukk 516); this synagogue was destroyed during Trajan's reign (98-117).

Tannaitic texts reflect the existence of a synagogue within the Jerusalem temple precinct in the stone-cutters' portico (M Yom 7,1; Sot 7,7-8). This synagogue appears to have been a place for reading of the Law (*bet ha-sefer*) and also a house of study (*bet*

35

ha-midraš). According to the Talmud (BT Sot 40b; Yom 68b), the High Priest read the Law there and recited blessings. Perhaps it is in this synagogue that the scene from the Gospels should be set, when the child Jesus was found by His parents «sitting in the midst of the doctors, both hearing them and asking them questions» (Lk 2:46).

A passage from the Palestinian Talmud (Meg 73d) speaks of 480 synagogues in Jerusalem which were destroyed by Vespasianus. Another from the Babylonian Talmud (Ket 105a) gives the figure of 394 synagogues and schools related to the 394 tribunals that existed in Jerusalem. Although some researchers reject these numbers as exaggerated, we should bear in mind that the archeological remains that have been discovered indicate the existence of small synagogues, which would explain such a high number. Tannaitic sources mention a synagogue in Tiberias as the scene of a heated halakhic controversy (M Šek 2,8).

The number of synagogues in Tiberias grew in the third century, after Judah the First, the Prince, established his seat and academy there. Tradition has it that there were thirteen synagogues and some of them belonged to groups of foreigners (BT Meg 30b). Likewise, the second city in Galilee, Sephoris, where Judah I established his seat for some time, had a similar number of synagogues in the third century. There was a «great synagogue» there, mentioned in Tannaitic sources, and it imitated temple worship on fasting days (Tos Ta'an 1,10). Seforis also had synagogues for groups of foreigners.

Philo and Flavius Josephus

Philo states that in Alexandria there were numerous synagogues in different suburbs of the city (*De Leg.* 132ff). Philo also refers to synagogues in Rome (*De Leg.* 156), from which at least thirteen inscriptions have been found (Baron, *Community*). Flavius Josephus mentions two synagogues which took part in incidents in the last Jewish uprising against Rome: the one at Caesarea, where its profanation, carried out by the Greek population in the city, marked the beginning of the Jewish uprising (66 A.D.) (Josephus, *Bell*

2,14,4-5); and the great *proseukhê* in Tiberias, an ample building with capacity for a large crowd. It was here that the party hostile to Flavius Josephus organized political assemblies using the pretext of fasting ceremonies (*De Vita Mos.* 44-45). Another synagogue mentioned by him is one at Dora (*Ant.* 19,305).

One conclusion is evident: the synagogue appears as a consolidated institution as from the first century of our era not only in Israel but also in the Diaspora.

For some time, temple and synagogue coexisted, with a close relationship. With the destruction of the temple and consequent end of sacrificial worship, the synagogue became the centre of Jewish religious life. Many of the temple practices and rites were deliberately transferred to the synagogue and others were prohibited precisely because they belonged exclusively to the Temple. Prayer was considered a substitute for sacrifices, and there was no obstacle or impediment in the word *'Abodah,* which had been used to refer to the sacrificial system, being applied now to prayer, which became the *'Abodah* from the heart (Sif Dt 41).

CHAPTER II

ARCHAEOLOGICAL EVIDENCE
OF ANCIENT SYNAGOGUES

1. EARLIEST ARCHAEOLOGICAL EVIDENCE

Bearing in mind the need felt by Jews in the Diaspora for places of worship and the difficulty of travelling to the temple at Jerusalem, it is easy to understand why it is precisely in the Diaspora, and particularly in Egypt, where archaeological evidence of the first or oldest synagogues has appeared.

> In Egypt there existed the temples of Elephantine and of Onias, but they did not have the sentimental hold exercised by the Jerusalem Temple.

The first archaeological evidence of the existence of a synagogue is an inscription discovered in 1902 in Shedia, 26 kilometres from Alexandria, a marble slab stating that the Jews dedicated this synagogue to Ptolemy III Euergetes (246-221 B.C.) and his queen, Berenice. The inscription mentions the *proseukhê* (prayer-house of prayer?) and the Jews, so it is evident that at this time the synagogue was an institution already long established. From the same period and country is a dedicatory inscription found in Lower Egypt guaranting rights of asylum to the synagogue. The mention in 3 Mc 7:20 of the founding of a synagogue at Ptolemais during the reign of Ptolemy IV (221-204 B.C.) is therefore feasible. Later evidence dates from 37 B.C. and comes from an inscription of Theodotus, son of Vetenus, found on Mount Ophel to the south-east of Jerusalem, with the following text: «Theodotus, son of Vetenus, priest and archisynagogos, grandson of an archysinagogos, built this synagogue for the reading of the Law and for the teaching of the

39

commandments and the guest house and rooms and supplies of water as an inn for those who are in need when coming from abroad, which synagogue his fathers and the elders and Simonides founded».

This inscription appears to refer to a synagogue belonging to a group of foreigners, possibly pilgrims from Rome. The titular head, Theodotus, could be identified as Theudas, the head of Roman Jewry and deeply respected also in Palestine for his generous aid to students and scholars of the Law. Hence he would be the most qualified patron of a synagogue whose explicit aim was «the reading of the Law and teaching of the commandments». This seems to be the synagogue that is referred to in the Acts of the Apostles (6:9) when speaking of Stephen's dispute with certain members of the synagogue of the Libertines, from Cyrenia, Alexandria, Cilicia and Asia.

In the synagogue at the Roman port of Ostia, from the third century A.D., some fragments have been found of an inscription from the second century A.D. which could point to the existence of a house of Jewish worship in that same place during Emperor Augustus' reign. It is also possible that the public buildings at Caesarea, from the first century B.C., and the ones in Tiberias from the first century A.D., discovered beneath the foundations of Palestinian synagogues, had also been used for Jewish cult, but clear archaeological proof is lacking. In the Masada excavations, in the Dead Sea, a building was found within an older construction which could possibly have been a synagogue erected by the Zealots when the Romans laid siege to the fortress from 66-73 A.D.

In addition, several Greek inscriptions casually mention parts of the synagogue building: an *exedra* in Atribis (Egypt); a *pronaos* in Mantinea and *a peribolos tou hypaithrou* in Focea (Ionic coast of Asia Minor), a fountain and patio in Side, a dining hall and quadruple portico in Stobi in Macedonia.

All the same, the first archaeological foundations of synagogue buildings in Palestine (Galilee), in Asia Minor (Miletus, Priene, Sardis) and Rome (near Ostia) date from the first century onwards of our times.

2. ANCIENT SYNAGOGUES IN PALESTINE

Architectural structure

Because of the purpose for which it was used, the synagogue clearly had to be different to the sanctuary. Whilst in the latter the only person who entered was the priest, with the rest of the worshipers at a distance, in the synagogue the centre around which the liturgy revolves is general participation in common prayer. Thus the synagogue building should have ample space inside to admit members of the community, making it possible for them to hear the readings from the Torah, see the chanter and be seated during religious services.

The architectural model most similar to the synagogue buildings were not the pagan sanctuaries from the Hellenistic Roman world but rather the Greek *bouleutêria* or *ekklesiastêria* in which large groups of people met and debated. Architecturally speaking, the model became more complicated, as a space had to be incorporated — the women's gallery — to enable their attendance at services. A basilica model was adopted, with columns around an open space and a gallery over inner porticos.

The development of the different types of synagogue building can mainly be traced in Palestine, where numerous archaeological remains of synagogues built between the first and eight centuries have been discovered.

Different types

These buildings can be classified in three types or groups: the *basilical* synagogue, the *broad-house* synagogue and the *apsidal* synagogue.

a) The *«basilical»* synagogue

The oldest type, represented in the synagogues of Galilee and Golan, was a building constructed with square hewn stones, elaborate facade, facing Jerusalem, with three doors. The interior was built on the lines of a typical Graeco-Roman basilica, prototype of

Syrian Roman and Nabatean buildings, with two rows of parallel columns and a third transversal row behind the doors. The columns were smooth and stood on high pedestals; the capitals were of simplified Corinthian style.

Contrasting with the ornate decoration of the facade, the interior, a hall with stone paving, was bereft of decoration except for a frieze round the upper gallery. This absence of decoration was deliberate to avoid distracting worshipers. The room received light through windows, mostly looking towards Jerusalem. The frieze usually presented an elongated garland of acanthus or bunches of grapes with bas-relief showing diverse pictures or symbols, like the *měnorah*, the *šofar*, *'etrog*, *lulab* and the holy Ark; there were also geometrical figures inside, like the hexagram (Shield of David) or the pentagram (Seal of Solomon) and the fruits of the land, in particular «the seven species», especially those quoted in the book of Deuteronomy (8:8): «a land of wheat, and barley, and vines, and fig trees and pomegranates; a land of oil olive and honey». Sometimes the tolerant attitude of the communities even allowed the inclusion of decorative patterns, lacking in pagan significance, mythological figures: a griffin and a capricorn, Hercules with his staff, a centaur, a Medusa, a human face or a vintage scene. Occasionally on the dintels of the synagogue the Roman emblem, an eagle, appeared. These motifs were all in relief, except the lions of Chorazin which were threedimensional. Very often a row of stone slabs ran along two or three sides of the synagogue's inner hall for seating.

The architects of these synagogues had probably studied at the architectural schools in Syria. From inscriptions we know the names of some of them, although it is not always clear if the person named was the architect or merely someone who donated the synagogue to the community.

The upper gallery ran parallel to three sides of the main hall, but not on the facade side. Although many scholars believe the gallery was used exclusively by women during religious ceremonies, nevertheless a recent investigator has shown with convincing arguments that women were not excluded from participating in worship together with the men during the Talmud period (cfr. E. Meyers, «Synagogue», *IDB*, supplement, page 843). This gallery was reached by a flight of steps outside the building. Some of these synagogues had an adjacent room to keep the Torah scrolls. Sometimes there was an adjoining patio surrounded by porticos used for resting during religious services or for wayfarers to sleep. As it was not yet the custom to construct a niche or shrine for the Torah scrolls, they were kept in a container or ark which was brought in when necessary. So the synagogue in this period had no niche for the scrolls, except the synagogue at Beth-Arbel (in Galilee) which has one on the main facade wall, but it is doubtful whether it belongs to the same period as the synagogue itself.

The size of these synagogues — about fifteen all told — varies from 360 square metres, the largest — at Capernaum — and 110, the smallest. The latter represents the average size of the synagogues found.

With slight variations, these basilical type synagogues date from the third and fourth centuries of our time. The synagogue at Capernaum and Chorazin are examples of this first type.

b) *The «broad-house» synagogue*

There is a second type of synagogues, called transitional, although excavations have shown that this denomination is erroneous, as some of them are prior to the basilical-synagogue prototype we have spoken of. In this second type various attempts were made to prevent the entrance and the dais or forum for worshipers from facing the same direction, that is, towards Jerusalem.

One solution was the synagogue at Eshtemoa in Judah, an amplified building — the so-named «broad-house» — of rectangular form with a niche for the Torah altar on the widest side of the rectangle orientated towards Jerusalem; the monumental facade with three doors, preceded by a portico with pillars was on the narrowest side of the building. Another example is the synagogue at Beth Shearim which was adapted from a building that already existed, shutting off the central door of the facade and preserving the two side doors as entrances. In this way a new setting was created for the place where the Torah scrolls were kept, facing Jerusalem. Of the two synagogues found in Hammat Tiberias, one, of basilica form, has its entrance on the north side and terminates on the narrow south side facing Jerusalem; later, a square room was added on the centre of the southern wall to serve as an ark for the Torah; above this fourth century addition another was built in the sixth century, in the centre of which was a little niche flanked by small pillars.

These synagogues — although not all of them — had a *bimah*, an elevated platform, surrounded by a railing for safety, and a niche for the Torah. The first synagogues with mosaic paving, substituting the stone slabs in earlier models, are from this period, like the one at Susiya. The mosaic paving had only geometrical patterns but as from the third century figures were permitted (according to a saying of R. Abin mentioned in the Jerusalem Talmud [A.Z. 3,4,42d]).

c) The «apsidal» synagogue

The third type of synagogue, of apsidal design, is represented by the Beth Alpha synagogue on the Jezrael plain. The synagogues at Gaza, Maon and Hammath Gader, among others, belong to this group. This new type of synagogue dates from the fifth to eighth centuries A.D. They were built to a Byzantine basilica plan, used in churches of the same period: the building had a large hall separated into central and side naves by two rows of pillars with ornate capitals, terminating in a semicircular apse pointing towards Jerusalem. They sometimes had an atrium and narthex.

Narthex is the place in Christian churches reserved for catechumens.

Entrance to the building was by way of three doors, situated on the opposite side to Jerusalem. The Torah altar was in the apse and the *bimah,* for the speakers, was opposite. At the further end of the apse was a space separated from the rest by a chancel screen with columns and chancel slabs. In this space there was sometimes a dark place, probably to comply with the verse: «Out of the depths have I cried unto thee, oh Lord. Lord, hear my voice» (Ps 130:1). Behind the apse was a cavity used for storage or to house deteriorated Torah scrolls (*gĕnizah*). The floor was profusely decorated with mosaics depicting Biblical episodes like Noah's ark or Isaac's sacrifice or Daniel in the lions' den.

44

In the synagogue at Hammath Tiberias we can see the prototype of these synagogues' paving, with the signs of the Zodiac, Helio the sun-god, in the centre of a circle, and the seasons in the four angles. The Zodiac circle was situated in the centre of the paving, and towards the end of the apse, an illustration of the ark of the Torah flanked by two *měnorot* or candelabra by its sides. The Zodiac in the paving, represented by a series of months and seasons was apparently lacking in idolatrous implications and a specifically Jewish interpretation was attributed. It was also to be found in the temple to indicate fixed feast days and the succession of the priests' *mismarot* and *ma'amadot*.

Another example of this type of synagogue is to be found at Nirim; in its mosaic the pagan symbols of wine, peacocks and offerings were replaced at the critical spot, in front of the Torah altar, by purely Jewish symbols like the *měnorah, 'etrog, lulab* and *šofar*. In later synagogues of this type (Hammath Gader, Jericho and Ain-Gedi) a certain resistance to using live beings as decorative motifs can be observed: in Hammath there are only two lions, in Jericho no pictures at all. The only synagogues of this type inscribed with their date of construction are those at Gaza and Beth Alpha (518-27 A.D.). We do not know the names of their constructors, only those of the authors of the mosaics at Beth Alpha: a certain Marinos and his son Hananias. In the Samaritan synagogues, the decoration showed more austerity than those at Judah: only the ark of the Law and ornamental motifs of the flora of the land, as well as geometrical patterns.

The exterior of the building was simple, with no decoration, as these synagogues were erected in Byzantine times, when the construction of new synagogues was forbidden and existing ones were only allowed to be repaired when falling into ruin. Although this ruling was not strictly observed, certain precautions used to be taken.

On the outside there was usually a flight of steps to give access to the women's gallery. The synagogues of this period, although not identical in form, seem to have followed a common architectural model with slight variations.

Dating

The mosaic paving and the type of mosaic used are extremely important in order to date the ancient synagogues and determine their origin. Prior to the fourth century only floral or geometrical patterns were used in mosaic paving. In the same way as their Christian contemporaries, Jewish spiritual leaders refused to allow the introduction in religious buildings of any motif with the slightest trace of idolatry.

The acceptance of pictorial murals and mosaics in synagogues was due to R. Yohanan and R. Abin in the second half of the third century: in the *Pseudo Jonathan* Targum to Lv 26:1 it is said: «You can put mosaic paving decorated with images and likenesses on the floor of your sanctuaries, but not to bow down unto».

As from the fourth century human figures appeared on mosaic paving, taking priority Biblical motifs in which Providence was revealed acting in moments of peril: Noah's ark, Daniel in the lions' den, etc.

Masada and Herodium (I century)

The only two synagogues in Palestine that belong to Jesus' time are one at Masada (on the eastern slopes of the Judah mountains, to the west of the Dead Sea) and another at Herodium (a few kilometres south-east of Bethlehem). In the Masada synagogue two periods can be observed. In its original form it consisted of a rectangular building fifteen metres by twelve, with two rows of columns. The paving was of grey plaster. The entrance was on the eastern wall; the main hall was reached by way of an atrium. The Zealots introduced various structural alterations, removing two pillars and a wall and installing graded benches of plastered stone along the walls. The Herodian construction plan is similar to that of various synagogues in Galilee. The synagogue discovered at Herodium is of similar characteristics. However, as it was a reconverted Herodian palace chamber (during the first Jewish uprising the occupants of the fortress installed benches along the walls and a ritual bath nearby) this discovery seems less significant than that at Masada, where the chamber in question seems to have been built originally for religious purposes.

Other synagogues

Finally we offer the datation of other ancient synagogues: Beth Shean (VI century); Capernaum (according to some, roughly towards the end of the fourth and beginning of the fifth centuries; others maintain towards the end of the third, beginning of fourth centuries); Chorazin (I-II? centuries); Gerash in Transjordania (prior to 530, as in that year a church was built in that place, over the ruins of the synagogue); Gaza (aprox. 508-509 according to an inscription) and Beth Alpha (in time of Emperor Justinus I who reigned from 518 to 527).

CHAPTER III

THE SYNAGOGUE IN THE MISHNA, TALMUD AND RABBINIC TEXTS FROM THE FIRST CENTURIES OF OUR ERA

In the Mishna there is no tractate specifically dedicated to the synagogue. The pertinent legislation is almost entirely limited to the *Měgillah* tractate where hardly anything is regulated about its emplacement, orientation or architecture. The few ancient rules to this respect come from the *Tosephta'*, compiled mostly from remains of ancient laws and customs — very often repudiated — combined with tradition posterior to the Mishna. For lack of other regulation, the Mishna enjoys *ipso facto* authority.

> *Měgillah* means volume or scroll, from the form of the ancient books, made up of various pieces of papyrus, sewn together one after another, in such a way that once each end was fixed to rods or cylinders they could be rolled round them, especially when the scrolls were voluminous (cf. Is 34:4; Zech 5:1ff; Ps 40:8). Five *měgillot* or volumes are read in the synagogue throughout the liturgical year: The Song of Songs (at Passover), Ruth (Pentecost), Lamentations (the ninth day of the month of Av, commemorating the destruction of the temple), Ecclesiastes (feast of the Tabernacles) and Esther (feast of *Purim*). The order listed dates from the twelfth century. Of the five, the Esther scroll is the *Měgillah* par excellence.
>
> The *Měgillah* contains instructions relating to the reading of the book of Esther at the *Purim* or feasts of lots, as well as other literary and liturgical indications.

1. SACREDNESS OF THE SYNAGOGUE AND ITS UTENSILS

Although the synagogue does not have the same sacred implications as the Temple, the rabbis attributed it with a similar sanctity, considering it second only to the great spiritual centre represented by the temple.

The synagogues in the Diaspora were as sacred as those in Palestine, as they were considered part of the land, as extra-territorial emplacements abroad; according to the Talmud, «in times to come the Babylonian synagogues would be transferred to Israel» (BT Meg 29a). The verse from Ez 11:16: «Yet will I be to them as a little sanctuary... in the countries where they shall come». And one sage even went so far as to say that «God is to be found in the synagogue» (BT Ber 6a) despite the fact that traditional rabbinical theology maintains that «all the land is full of His glory» according to Is 6:4. Another sage applied Ps 90:1 to the synagogue: «Lord, thou hast been our dwelling-place in all generations.»

The synagogue and its utensils have a sacred nature, so they can only be traded in commercial transactions with superior entities or objects. A text from the Mishna says: «If the people have sold a site, with its price a synagogue shall be bought; if a synagogue be sold, an ark shall be bought; if an ark be sold, cloths to cover the Torah scrolls shall be bought; if cloths, rolls (rods round which to roll the Torah text); if rolls, with their price a Torah shall be bought; but if a Torah is sold, with its price rods for the Torah shall not be bought; if rods, cloths shall not be bought; if cloths to cover the Torah, an ark shall not be bought; and if a synagogue be sold, with its price a site shall not be bought» (M Meg 3, 1). From this text it is clear that the container (the synagogue) is inferior to any thing contained (ark, Torah cylinders, etc.) but superior to any other exterior reality (site).

The most sacred object in the synagogue is the Torah scrolls, the nearer the rest of the objects are to them, the greater their degree of sacredness. This sacred scale, if we can call it such, should be respected so that an object may never serve for an inferior use to the one it was designed for: an ark rejected for Torah use, for example, should not be made into a chair, although the opposite can be done.

R. Eleazar stated that a site where a synagogue had stood should not be sold unless it were to build another in its place (PT Ned 41c). R. Judah said: «No funeral prayers shall be said in a synagogue in ruins; no lines shall be hung there; no snares be set; no fruit

50

shall be dried on its roof; it shall not be used as a passage, according to what is said (Lv 26:31)» (M Meg 3,3).

«Synagogues are still sacred, even when they have been abandoned; if grass grows over them, it should be respected as a sign of grief and not be pulled up» (M Meg 3,3). The synagogues should be respected, almost as much as the Jerusalem Temple: «No lightness will be permitted in them; and they shall not be entered to shelter from the sun, the cold or the rain; neither to eat, nor to drink; nor to sleep; nor to stroll nor to play. But in them (the Torah) can be read, studied and explained and public mourning can be done» (Tos Meg 3, 7). In the synagogue «behaviour such as the following is prohibited: frivolity, murmuring, eating, drinking, adorning oneself, sleeping or nodding off, entering with unsheathed knife, sheltering from bad weather, trading or praising anyone, unless he be a distinguished citizen» (Š Ar OH 151). «One can run into the synagogue but on leaving it is necessary to walk slowly so as not to give the impression of wanting to leave» (BT Ber 6b). R. Eleazar ben Shammua said he had lived to such a great age because he never used the synagogue as a short cut (BT Meg 27b).

Objects that have been used for synagogue worship and have become deteriorated, can be thrown away, except for those that have been consecrated; these should be put into a *gĕnizah* or dark chamber; examples of the former are the *lulab*, a trumpet, fringes, a tent or hut; examples of the latter are fragments of scrolls, phylacteries, *mĕzuzot*, the Torah scrolls' case, the phylacteries' case and their straps (BT Meg 26b).

> *Gĕnizah* (from Aramaean *gnz;* to be precious, hidden) is the chamber in the synagogue where the Jews were obliged to deposit the manuscripts from sacred books that were no longer usable for liturgy, in order that they be buried after a certain time in holy land and to preserve them meanwhile from all profanation or corruption.

The great esteem in which the rabbis held the synagogue was mainly due to the role it had played in keeping the community united and in perpetuating the Jewish people.

The Talmud homilies frequently call for synagogue attendance: «A man's prayer is only heard in the synagogue» (BT Ber 6a); «a person who does not attend the synagogue when there is one in his town is a bad neighbour (cf Jer 12:14) and brings exile upon himself and his children» (BT Ber 8a). Moreover «he who usually attends the synagogue and absents himself one days causes inquire on himself»; «God's wrath is roused when he finds no *quorum* at the synagogue» (cf Is 50:2; BT Ber 6a). One sage attributes «the longevity of the Babylonian Jews to their attending the synagogue and another recommends praying while the synagogue service is being held and one is unable to attend» (BT Ber 7a, 8a).

2. EMPLACEMENT OF THE SYNAGOGUE

Close by water

In the first century of our era the synagogue used to be erected close to water, following the Jewish custom of saying prayers by rivers or on the beach (Philo, *In Flacc.* 14). Josefo speaks of the custom of the Hellenistic Jewish communities «who built their places of worship by the sea» *(Ant.* 14, 258). The book of the Acts of the Apostles (16:13) refers to a Jewish place of prayer by a river: «And on the Sabbath we went out of the city by a river side, where prayer was wont to be made; and we sat down, and spake unto the women which rested thither.» With respect to the ancient synagogues in Palestine, the one at Capernaum is by the lakeside and the Caesarea one on the beach.

This fact reflects the ancient belief in the presence of God in water, which would later be rationalized by the explanation that the Jews needed abundant water for ablutions prior to worship (Acts 16:13). According to Josefo, «the people of Halicarnaso decreed that the Jews could build their places of worship near the sea, as was their native custom» *(Ant.* 14, 10, 23).

According to other writers, the synagogues in the diaspora should be built close to water where the land would be less contaminated.

52

The synagogue should be on the most elevated place in the city and so be its highest building (Tos Meg 4, 22-23). This is what is referred to in Prv 1:20-21 where it says textually: «Wisdom crieth without; She uttereth her voice in the streets: She crieth in the chief place of concourse, in the opening of her gates.» To all events this rule reflects the Biblical and oriental custom of placing sanctuaries on hills or high places. The temple at Jerusalem itself, towards which the synagogue or niche for the Torah ark used to face, was high on a hill. According to this, many of the ancient synagogues were situated on hills or mountains. Of the two synagogues at Gush Halav, a city in Upper Galilee, one was erected on the top of the hill where the city itself was built, the other in a valley by a fountain. The synagogue at Chorazim is in the centre of the city and at its highest point.

3. HEIGHT

According to Rav (year 245) «any city which has roofs higher than the synagogue will finally be destroyed, as it is written to set up the house of our God (Ezr 9:9)» (BT Šab 11a).

Of the ancient synagogues in Palestine the one at Capernaum was built on an artificial platform in the central, dominating part of the city. The roofs of the houses next to the east and south sides of the synagogue hardly reached the level of its stone paving. The custom continued until the Middle Ages. We know that halfway through the thirteenth century the archdeacon and ecclesiastical chapter, shortly after the reconquest of the city of Córdoba by Ferdinand III in 1235-1236, raised their voices in protest at the «excessive height» of the synagogue being built again by the Jews in Córdoba. This protest gave rise to a Papal bull from Innocence IV, published in Lyons on 13th April 125), ordering the diocesan bishop to discharge the duties of his post and, without appeal, take the appropriate measures with respect to the synagogue under construction that was causing «grave scandal to devote Christians and detriment to the Córdoba Church», breaking the law then in force on new buildings of this type (F. Cantera, *Sinagogas,* 4). In the Middle Ages, on the occasions when it was not possible to build a synagogue of larger dimensions than the surrounding houses, the practice was to set up a mast or girder on the roof that would rise above the neighbouring buildings.

4. ORIENTATION

The synagogue's orientation was determined from the beginning by the principle of the praying person's position. In the Talmud we can read the following: «Those who are without the land of Israel should turn their heart (= mind; PT: face) towards the land of Israel; those who are in Israel shall turn their heart towards Jerusalem, and in Jerusalem towards the Temple... Consequently, those who are to the north of Jerusalem will turn to face the south; those who are in the south, to the north; those in the west, to the east, so that the whole of Israel pray (facing) towards the same place» (Tos Ber 3, 15-16).

The Jerusalem temple stood on the south-east of the city, next to the Ophel Hill or City of David, near the place occupied today by the Omar sanctuary or Dome of the Rock (*Qubbet as-Sakhra*). Destroyed in 586 B.C. by the Babylonians, it was later restored by Ezra on returning from exile (536 B.C.); finally it was built to a new pattern during Herod's reign (37-4 B.C.) and destroyed by Tito's Roman legions in A.D. 70. The containing wall of the platform on which it was raised still remains as a witness to its existence, called today the Western Wall (*kotel ha-ma'ăraví*) or Wailing Wall (because the Jews have always come to it to pray and lament its destruction and still do so.

The period prior to the Jews being deported to Babylonia is called of First Temple Period and the one posterior to the exile, of the Second Temple Period.

Indeed, most of the ancient synagogues to be found in west-Jordania, to the north of Jerusalem, face south, while those in Trans-Jordania, a region situated to the east of Jerusalem, face west. The orientation principle seems to be based on I Kgs 8:22-30 in which Solomon prays before the altar of the Lord on the day of the temple's dedication, and on the book of Daniel (6:11) where he prays «his windows being open in his chamber towards Jerusalem».

54

The Talmud gives express instructions to face Jerusalem when the *'Ámidah* prayer is being said (BT Ber 30a).

The opinion is held that the wall opposite the synagogue's entrance should be orientated towards Jerusalem, so that worshipers, on entering the synagogue, would be facing Jerusalem (Tos Ber 3, 15-16).

This spatial arrangement, which predominated in the Middle Ages, continues to be prevalent up to our days.

It must be observed, however, that the ancient Palestinian synagogues were of two types: some with the entrance door on the main façade, facing Jerusalem, others with the entrance towards Jerusalem. In either case, worshipers faced Jerusalem during their prayers, so in the first case (that is, with the entrance door facing Jerusalem) once inside the synagogue they had to turn to face Jerusalem. Perhaps the reason is that the first synagogues had no niche to hold the Torah scrolls; when this was incorporated into the synagogue, the ark was placed facing Jerusalem, and in order to prevent worshipers entering the synagogue — the main door faced Jerusalem — with their backs to the Torah niche which also faced Jerusalem, the situation of the door was changed, placing it opposite Jerusalem. From that moment on, the main façade no longer determines the direction, but instead, the emplacement of the ark.

In any case, wherever it is possible, direct entrance from the street to the synagogue praying chamber will be avoided, by the use of a patio or entrance hall (BT Ber 8a) where there was a pool for hand (and foot) ablutions. Judah Loew b. Bezalel (Maharal) from Prague gave the explanation that worldly thoughts and preoccupations should be abandoned before entering the sacred sanctuary.

However, others feel that «the synagogue door should be on the eastern side, where the tabernacle had its entrance» (Nm 3:38; Tos Meg 4, 22). According to this, the west seems to be the principle for orientation and not that of Jerusalem and its temple. Nevertheless, this seems to have been the rule in the synagogues in Babylonia to the east of Palestine, so that synagogues built according to this orientation would face Palestine and the Jerusalem Temple. To all events, this custom reflects the posture of one sector of the Jews who identified the synagogue with the meeting tent.

The «meeting or testimony tent» was the portable sanctuary in the desert, which contained the ark of the covenant, considered as the dwelling place of Yahweh among His people.

The «ark of the covenant or of the Torah» was a wooden box containing, apparently, the table of the Law, where the decalogue was engraved (Dt 10:1ff; I Kgs 8:9). It was deposited in the holy of holies in Solomon's temple and overlaid with gold plate, the mercy seat (Ex 25:17-21) or *kapporet* (originally «that covers sins»; later «that removes sins»). This beaten gold was decorated with two cherubim, and placed above and over the holy of holies ark. It was the seat of divine presence and place of pardon by Yahweh through the sprinkling of sacrificial blood by the High Priest the Day of Atonement (*Yom Kippur*). It was supposed that Yahweh sat over these two cherubim; it was forbidden to represent his image. The Biblical expressions to refer to Yahweh as Thou that dwelleth among the cherubim and in the secret place of the most High (Ps 80:2; 91:1) come from here. In the Canaan world, kings were shown sitting on a chair supported by two cherubim, which the divinity used to move from one place to another.

5. DIMENSIONS

The dimension of the ancient synagogues ranges between 360 square metres, the largest — at Capernaum — and 110, the smallest, which reflects the average size. We can say that the synagogues in general were quite small, and this is the reason for their numerous presence in large cities. In the one at Dura Europos in Mesopotamia there was room for about fifty five men and thirty five women.

6. WINDOWS

The synagogue should have windows, according to Daniel 6:11: «Now when Daniel knew that the writing was signed, he went into his house; and his windows being open in his chamber towards Jerusalem, he kneeled upon his knees three times a day, and prayed, and gave thanks before his God, as he did aforetime.» The Talmud forbids praying in a room without windows (BT Ber 34b) and the *hălakah* decrees that «the synagogue should have 12 windows, onc for each of the twelve tribes of Israel»,' although this has rarely been put into practice literally (Š Ar OH 90, 4). Raši commented that «the windows were necessary to allow those who were praying to look towards the heavens, a posture that inspires reverence and devotion during prayers» (BT Ber 34b). If a wall were built in front of the synagogue's windows, it should be demolished, but this was not all: the normal requisite not to build nearer than six feet (about one and a half metres) from the synagogue's walls was insufficient because the synagogue needs plenty of light (Š Ar OH 150, 4).

7. FURNITURE, ADORNMENTS AND OTHER OBJECTS

The ark of the Torah

The essential piece of furniture in a synagogue was the ark, a coffer or box where one or two Torah scrolls were carefully stored and probably some of the Prophets' or *Haftarah* scrolls, to be read on the Sabbath and feast days. The ark of the Torah in Hebrew was called *tebah*, *'aron* and sometimes *'ăron ha-kodeš* (holy ark); in Aramaean, *tebuta'* or *'ărona'* (BT Šab 32a).

According to the Talmud, the expression *'ăron ha-kodeš* (holy ark), imposed by Jewish authorities, was not accepted at first by the people (BT Šab 32a).

The Torah scrolls were wrapped in linen cloths (*mtphwt*) and stored in cases (heb. *tyq;* gr. *thêkê*). The book of the Torah or Law was rolled round two rods or wooden cylinders called «the tree of life» (in Hebrew *'eṣ hayyim*).

Rabbinical sources call the ark *tebah,* an abbreviation of *tebah šel sĕfarim* (ark or coffer for books). This name refers to Gen 6:14 (LXX *kibôtos*), Ex 2:3 (LXX *thibin*); *thibin* is a Greek adaptation of the Hebrew term *tebah* and goes back to the second century B.C.

The term *'aron* (ark) refers to the ark in the meeting tent in the desert (Ex 25:10; Nm 10:35-36; 14:44 and others) and rarely appears in rabbinical texts.

57

A lamp burns constantly before the Ark (in Hebrew, *ner tamid*).

Researchers coincide in stating that the ark of the Torah did not have a fixed place in the synagogue until the third century or beginning of the fourth, but for security reasons was stored after religious services away from the synagogue or in an adjoining room, being brought into the synagogue when needed for worship. This fact seems to be confirmed by excavations. Only one of the ancient synagogues — the one at Arbel — has a niche for the Torah, and in all probability it does not correspond to the original building but was incorporated at a later date. The first synagogue in which a niche for the Torah ark appears is the one at Dura Europos (245 A.D.). When the synagogue begins to be considered as second to the Jerusalem temple it is necessary to find a permanent place for the ark, as it enjoyed in the temple. Some conservative Jewish circles, scandalized by this, reacted calling the ark «coffin», which in Hebrew is *'aron*. When opposition to this term died down, and the ark was installed permanently in the synagogue, this name prevailed for the box containing the Torah scrolls. In the same way as the ark of the tabernacle, the Torah ark was also covered and concealed from worshipers' eyes by the *paroket* (Hebrew) or *parokta* (Aramaean), veil or curtain which concealed the niche where the holy ark rested, or with the *killah,* a kind of mantle or canopy extended over the ark.

The «bimah» or tribune

Close by, in front of the Torah ark, was the *bimah* or dais used for the reading of the Torah or Prophets and for the giving of certain blessings, imitating the biblical scene when Ezra the scribe stood upon a pulpit of wood and «opened the book in the sight of all the people, for he was above the people» (Neh 8:4-5). On this pulpit a lectern was placed. Both items are mentioned in the Palestinian Talmud (PT 73d) and might have existed already in New Testament times.

The *bimah* was a platform, normally elevated, surrounded by a wooden safety rail, and it was from here that the Law and the Prophets were read and explained (Š Ar OH 150, 5). The *bimah* was situated near the ark, sometimes in the centre of the synagogue when the latter was large, like the one at Alexandria (Tos Sukk 4, 6).

The New Testament makes no mention of the *bimah,* although some see a reference to it in Matthew (23:2): «The scribes and the pharisees sit in Moses' seat...»

A Tannaitic tradition refers to the existence of a wooden bimah placed ad hoc in the atrium of the temple for Agripa I to read the Law on the Sukkoth Feast. The Mishna says: «This is the rite that corresponds to the part to be recited by the king. At the end of the first feast day (*Sukkot*) in the eighth year at the end of the sabbatical year, a wooden pulpit is raised in a yard and the king sits according to Dt 31:10. The minister of the synagogue takes the book of the Torah and passes it to the chief of the priests, and he gives it to the High Priest who hands it to the king: the king receives it and, seated, reads. King Agripa stood up to receive and read it, and the sages praised him. When the king reached the passage "one from among thy brethren shalt though set king over thee, which is not thy brother" (Dt 17:15) tears fell from his eyes; he was told "fear not Agripa, thou art our brother, thou art our brother, thou art our brother". And he read from the beginning of Deuteronomy (these be the words...) as far as "Hear" (= *Šema*ʻ), then he read the *Šema*ʻ and Dt 11:13, the statutes on tithes (Dt 14:22; 26:12) and the section on the king (Dt 17:14); then the blessing and maledictions till the end of the section. The king read the blessings the High Priest recites, although he gave the blessing relating to feasts instead of the one for the pardoning of sins» (M Sota 7,8).

In the third century, on the occasion of a visit by a famous preacher and sage, the placing of a high *bimah* in the Simonia (Palestine) synagogue is mentioned (PT Yeb 12,13a; Gen Rabbah 81,2). This *bimah* is a portable pulpit for reading; as a permanent marble or wooden structure it is referred to in a statement by Samuel (a Babylonian rabbi from the third century): «The *bimah* and planks are not as sacred as the ark, but only as much as the building.»

On the *bimah* was a lectern or desk used by the reader to support the Torah scrolls, and called *kursya'* o *'ănlagin* (lit. throne) in Hebrew and *analogeion* (lectern) in Greek (BT Meg 26b).

Today the *bimah* is also called *al-Memar,* of Arabic origin it is a shortened form of the Arab expression *al-Mimbar* used to refer to the chair or pulpit used for Friday preachings in the mosque.

The modern custom of placing the pulpit or *bimah* to the fore of the synagogue in order to leave more room free for the people who attend found great opposition at the beginning (Š Ar OH 150, 5). In 1886 the rabbis in Hungary and Wales declared *herem* (excommunication) to punish this practice. To all events, the habit took root, especially in the United States of America, even among orthodox Jews who explained it away quoting Joseph Caro's opinion that the *bimah*'s position could be altered according to the time and the place (Sepher Mishna to Yad, Tef 11,3).

As well as the *bimah,* there was a special place in the synagogue for the person who led the prayers. This was sometimes below floor level; as the ark was placed on high, the Talmud describes the person who leads prayer as being underneath, before the ark (Heb. *yored liphne ha-tebah*) (BT Taan 2,2).

The seats

Some of the ancient synagogues had stone benches along the walls; in Hebrew they were called *safsalim* (sing. *safsal*) or *kliterah;* in Greek, *sypsellion* or *klintêr* (PT Meg 73d); usually however, people used to sit on the floor or remain standing. Matthew the evangelist (23:7) speaks of seats of honour (*prôtokathedría*) for the most important persons. It appears that in Babylonia in the third century mats were placed on the floor for people to sit on (Heb. *sifa'; mahsalot*) (BT Meg 73d). The seat of highest honour, no doubt destined for the use of the synagogue's president, was known as «the seat» or «Moses' chair». Many of them have been discovered, for example in Chorazim, in Hammat (near Tiberias) and in Delos.

The seats nearest the ark, facing the assembly, were reserved for the elders (Š Ar OH 150, 5). This arrangement gave rise to the general desire to sit near the eastern wall — *kotel mizrahi* — as the most ideal place in the synagogue. So the seats were arranged according to a certain order, with the most distinguished members of the congregation in the first rows and the youngest at the back.

Philo says that the Essenes used to be seated according to age, the youngest «below» (that is behind) the eldest.

In the Qumran regulations for assemblies and solemn meals a hierarchical order is established similar to the seating one: This is the rule for the congregation assembly: every man shall sit in his place. The priest shall be seated first and the rest of the people according to their category (1QS 6,89). In the Synagogue at Alexandria the men sat separately, according to their crafts (PT Sukk 55ab); if there were a leper among the congregation a special compartment was set aside for him (PT Neg 13,12; Meg 4,3).

Candelabra and lamps

To light the synagogue one or more candelabra (Heb. *měnorot)* with lamps (Heb. *nerot)* were used. The candelabrum was called *měnorah,* a Hebrew word, derived from *nur* (light). The *měnorah* is used in the NT as a technical term to refer to the candelabrum with seven branches, used in the meeting tent and later in the temple. Ex 25:31-40 describes the gold candelabrum with seven branches: «And thou shalt make a candlestick of pure gold: of beaten work shall the candlestick be made: his shaft, and his branches, his bowls, his knops, and his flowers, shall be of the same. And six branches shall come out of the sides of it; three branches of the candlestick out of the one side, and three branches of the candlestick out of the other side: three bowls made like unto almonds, with a knop and a flower in one branch; and three bowls made like almonds in the other branch, with a knop and a flower: so in the six branches that come out of the candlestick. And in the candlestick shall be four bowls made like unto almonds, with their knops and their flowers. And there shall be a knop under two branches of the same, and a knop under two branches of the same, and a knop under two branches of the same, according to the six branches that proceed out of the candlestick. Their knops and their branches shall be of the same; all it shall be one beaten work of pure gold. And thou shalt make the seven lamps thereof: and they shall light the lamps thereof, and they may give light over against it. And the tongs thereof, and the snuffdishes thereof, shall be of

61

pure gold. Of a talent of pure gold shall he make it, with all these vessels. And look that thou make them after their pattern, which was shewed to thee in the mount» (cf. also Ex 37:17-24).

The book of Leviticus refers to the candelabrum, whose lamps should burn constantly before Yahweh in these terms: «And the Lord spake unto Moses, saying, Command the children of Israel, that they bring unto thee pure olive oil beaten for the light, to cause the lamps to burn constantly. Without the vail of the testimony, in the tabernacle of the congregation, shall Aaron order it from the evening unto the morning before the Lord continually: it shall be a statute for ever in your generations. He shall order the lamps upon the pure candlestick before the Lord continually» (Lv 24:3). Zechariah (4:2-11) describes his vision of the candelabrum in these terms: «I have looked, and behold a candlestick all of gold, with a bowl upon the top of it, and his seven lamps thereon, and seven pipe to the seven lamps, which are upon the top thereof...»

Rabbinic sources consider the best gift for a synagogue to be a *mĕnorah* (PT Tos Meg 74a). In the decoration of the oldest synagogues, the *mĕnorah* does not occupy an important place; but it does in the synagogue at Dura-Europos in Babylonia where, together with the ark, it is a motive of dominant decoration, especially adorning the niche or tabernacle of the Ark. Later the *mĕnorah* would become a prominent object of decoration in Palestinian synagogues, under the influence of the Babylonian synagogues. A fine example is to be found in the one at Hammat Tiberias whose mosaic contains candelabra surrounding the Ark of the Torah. In this synagogue a stone candelabrum designed to support seven ceramic lamps has also been found.

The horn, the trumpet, the «lulab» and the «'etrog»

Other utensils used on certain occasions in the synagogue are the horn, the trumpet, the *lulab* and the *'etrog.*

Horn and trumpet

The curved horn of a ram was used as a musical instrument. This instrument was called *qeren ha-yobel* in Hebrew (lit. ram's horn: Jos 6:5; cf I Chr 25,5). Using it as a trumpet, *yoḇel* (which originally means ram) took on the meaning of trumpet. Trumpet is *ḥăṣoṣrah* in Hebrew; in Greek *salpigx*. Pictures of these musical instruments are to be found on mosaics in synagogues and Jewish catacombs.

The horn is blown on New Year's day and the trumpet on fasting days (M Ta'an 2,3). Josephus Flavius calls the New Year's feast, the trumpet feast (Gr. *salpigges; De Spec. Leg.* I, 35 [186]; II, 31 [188]). The beginning and end of the Sabbath were announced by trumpet call so that people knew when to interrupt and when to renew their work.

The Mishna regulated the number of trumpet calls for different occasions: in the temple no less than 21 and no more than 48. Every day 21 calls were sounded: three to open the doors; nine for perpetual sacrifice in the morning and another nine for the evening one; new calls were added for additional sacrifices. On the eve of the Sabbath six calls were added: three to abandon work, three to mark the separation between what was sacred and what was profane. The eve of the Sabbath, during the feast of tents or tabernacles, 48 calls were sounded: three to open the doors, three for the upper door, and another three for the lower one and three to accompany the bringing of waters; three over the altar (for libations); nine for the morning perpetual sacrifice and another nine for the evening one, nine for additional sacrifices, nine to leave off work and three to mark the separation between what is divine and what is profane (M Sukk 5,5).

Likewise the Jubilee year (jubilee derives from *yoḇel*) was declared by the trumpet sounding (Lv 25:13ff; 27:18a,21; Nm 36:4). In the temple at Jerusalem the priests were in charge of this (BT Sukk 5,5; Josephus, *Bell.* 4,9,12 [582]).

«'Etrog» and «lulaḇ»

'Etrog is the citron which, together with the palm (*lulaḇ*) forms the ceremonial branch used for the *Sukkot* feast proclaiming these feast days sacred.

Lulaḇ is the palm which makes up the ceremonial branch for the *Sukkot* feast service, together with myrtle and willow leaves and the *'etrog* or citron.

The «mĕzuzah»

Mĕzuzah is a Hebrew word that means door posts, and from this, also door. It usually appears in plural (*mĕzuzot*) referring to the two door posts of the Israelites' houses in Egypt (Ex 12:7, 22-23) or to the houses they would inhabit in Palestine (Dt 6:9; 11:20), the posts of the doors in Gaza (Jgs 16:3), the door of the temple at Shiloh (I Sam 1:9), the posts at the entrance of Solomon's temple (I Kgs 6:33) or Ezekiel's (Ez 41:21; 43:8; 45:19).

The door posts, like the lintel, were consecrated and sprinkled with sacrificed animal blood on the celebration of the Passover (Ex 12:7,22-23); this rite — of pre-Israelite origin practised by nomadic shepherds who wanted to keep perils and disasters from their tents and families when setting off with their flocks in search of spring pasture — is used as a password by the Israelites the Exodus night so that the exterminator would pass by and not kill their first-born.

From the literal interpretation of Dt 6:6-9 and 11:18-20 (whose texts are very similar), it became the custom to place texts from the Scriptures on the door posts. Dt 6:6-9 reads: «And these words, which I command thee this day, shall be in thine heart: and thou shalt teach them diligently unto thy children, and shalt talk of them when thou sittest in thine house, and when thou walkest by the way, and when thou liest down, and when thou risest up. And thou shalt bind them for a sign upon thine hand, and they shall be as frontlets between thine eyes. And thou shalt write them upon the posts (*mĕzuzot*) of thy house, and on thy gates.»

And from here *mĕzuzah* came to mean a box, generally metal or wooden, fixed to the door posts of synagogues and Jewish houses, containing a small piece of parchment, on which 22 lines are written, the text from Dt 6:4-9 and 11:13-21, according to the prescription in Dt 6:6-9 and 11:18-20. On the reverse side of this parchment, rolled from left to right, God's name is written (*Šadday*). This name can be seen through a small window in the box. People leaving or entering the house almost always touch it with their fingers which they then kiss.

The *mĕzuzah* is fixed to the right post of the street door (BT Yom 10b ff) and occasionally, according to some, to the door posts

64

Mosaic paving in the Hammat synagogue in Tiberias, representing the ark of the Torah flanked by two candelabra and the signs of the zodiac

Foundation inscription at the Hammat synagogue, Tiberias

Herodium synagogue with stone benches along the sides

Watzinger's reconstruction of the Capernaum synagogue

of all the rooms. The use of the *mĕzuzah,* which stems from a literal interpretation of the texts quoted from the Scriptures was apparently first introduced after the exile, but it is not mentioned in either the Old or the New Testaments. The rabbi's prescriptions on the *mĕzuzah* are to be found in the seven short tracts added to the Palestinian Talmud.

In the Mishna (Men 29a-34a) several prescriptions are given on the *mĕzuzah;* one of them establishes that for the *mĕzuzah* to be valid both texts should be complete and correctly written, a badly written word makes it invalid.

According to the *Mekilta* to Exodus (12,24, p.39), the *mĕzuzah* has a protective value and is a guarantee against sin; in this context R. Eleazar ben R. Jacob stated: «Anyone who has the two phylacteries, fringes on his clothes, the *mĕzuzah* on his doors, is supposed not to sin, according to what is said» (Ecclo 4:12 and Ps 34:8). These two texts apply to the *mĕzuzah;* the first of them, Ecclo 4:12 refers to wisdom and says: «Those who love it, love life; those who seek it, find God's favour»; the second one says: «The angel of the Lord encampeth round about them that fear him, and delivereth them» (BT Men 43b). Putting the *mĕzuzah* at the door is a guarantee of divine protection.

On the back of the parchment that is inserted in the *mĕzuzah* in exactly the same place that corresponds to where the words *yahweh 'ēlohenu yahweh* (Yahweh, our God Yahweh) are written in the first line on the front, there is a row of letters, to show which is the back of the parchment scroll and prevent it being put into the box inside out. According to the cabbalistic alphabet system these letters are the ones in the Hebrew alphabet that respectively follow the letters of the words in the first line on the front; thus: *kwzw bmwksz kwzw;* and these letters on the back are written to coincide exactly with the letters on the front (so the order is reversed). Later interpretations have taken these letters to represent names of angels (Kuzu, Bemuksaz, Kuzu).

The synagogue used to belong to the local community; but it was sometimes private property or had been built by a person, or normally a group of people, who later donated it to the community. This partly explains the different sizes and decoration of the various ancient synagogues we know today.

As a general rule we can establish that the synagogue belongs to the community and to those who have contributed to its construction.

In small towns, where it was supposed that no outside donations were made towards the building of the local synagogue, the decision to sell is taken by the community or its representatives (M Ned 5,5); in cities the sale of the building was more difficult as it was not always possible to find out for sure if strangers had participated in its construction, and selling it without their consent would be an offense against their rights. This difficulty was solved by naming a rabbi who from the very beginning of the construction work would make decisions and these would be accepted by everyone, or he would be given full authority when the time came to sell.

To all events the demolishing of a synagogue was forbidden without having built a new one first, to avoid the community being without a synagogue meanwhile (BT B.B. 3b). It could only be sold if on the point of falling into ruins, on the condition that the construction of the new one commenced immediately (PT Ned 41c).

If a community decided to split a synagogue up into two, its objects should be divided proportionally between the members of both. But the rabbis argued whether women and children should be included in the count.

Whoever donated objects to the synagogue had the right to engrave his name on them. «Having given Antoninus a lamp holder to a synagogue, Rabbi said: "Blessed be the Lord who has put the idea into his heart of giving this lamp holder to the synagogue"» (PT Meg 74a).

With objects donated to the synagogue any other thing could

be bought, unless the object had its donor's name engraved on it (Tos Meg 3,3) and respecting the category of the object sold, so that it would not be exchanged for something less sacred or of lower value (M Meg 3,1).

CHAPTER IV

MEN, WOMEN, CHILDREN AND NON-JEWS IN THE SYNAGOGUE

1. WOMEN AND CHILDREN IN THE SYNAGOGUE

Various sources testify to the presence of women and children in the synagogue. According to the Mishna, «women, slaves and minors are not obliged to recite the *Šema'* or wear phylacteries; but they are obliged to pray, to install the *mĕzuzah* and to join in the blessing after meals» (M Ber 3,3).

Several *hălakot* take for granted the regular attendance of men, women and children at synagogue services. The Talmud forbids the Jews to eat any food cooked by a gentile. A baraita gives an exception to this rule: «An Israelite should not hesitate to leave food cooking on the fire allowing a gentile to stir it till he returns from the synagogue or from the *bet ha-midraš*. A woman should not hesitate to put a pot on the stove allowing a gentile to stir it until she returns from the baths or from the synagogue» (BT A.Z. 38b-39a). This law takes into account that the synagogue and the baths are places frequented also by women. The Talmud says: «In a town where all are priests, these should give the blessing. Whom should they bless? Their brothers to the north, south, east and west. But who will answer "Amen" to the priests? The women and children» (PT Ber 9d; cf BT Sot 38b). A late talmudical text, which undoubtedly reflects the normal custom says: «So it is correct to say that, after every passage from the Torah and the Prophets, read on the Sabbath, the translation should be read for the benefit of the people, including women and children. That is what is meant by: "come early and leave late on the Sabbath". Pious people should arrive early to join in the reciting of the *Šema'*, before sunrise. They leave late, in order to listen to the explanation of the Scripture. But on feast days they arrive late because they must prepare the meal for the feast day» (Sof 18,6). The *hălakah* explains why: women arrive early on the Sabbath because cooking is forbidden; late on feast days, because they have to prepare the meal, which is permitted on feast days.

The texts quoted are later than 70 A.D. but women attending the synagogue is undoubtedly earlier than that date, as can be seen from the text in Acts 16:11-15 when Paul and Timotheus went out of the city by a riverside, where prayer was wont to be made and spake unto the women which resorted thither.

Women and children formed part of the community but did not officiate or read at religious services. The Talmud says: «All may attend to complete the quorum of seven, even women and children. But the sages say a woman may not read the Scripture out of respect for the congregation» (BT Meg 23a; Tos Meg 4,11).

But if it is true to say that women and children attended the synagogue regularly, we cannot state with the same certainty that they followed synagogue worship spatially together with or apart from the men.

2. THE SEPARATION OF MEN AND WOMEN

The earliest rabbinical sources contain no legislation on the separation of men and women at the ancient Palestinian synagogues.

The separation was, however, a rule in the temple at Jerusalem, built by Herod. This temple had several atriums: the inner one or priests' separated from the Israelites' (or men's) and from the women's and the latter were to remain here and could not enter the one reserved for men. The women's courtyard was surrounded by a thick wall with several magnificent doors, among them the Beautiful (in Greek *hôraia*) or Golden Gate, as it also used to be called owing to an incorrect interpretation of *hôraia* (from Greek, «beautiful») for *aurea* (from Latin, «golden»). The gate mentioned in Acts 3:2 gave onto the Cedron brook and Mount of Olives.

From the *Sukkah* tractate, which regulates the *Sukkot* or tabernacle feast, we know that this separation of men and women is possibly based on the *Great Promulgation* (Heb. *tiqqun gadol)* or separation decree for men and women on the *Sukkot* feast during the ceremony in which a priest brought water in a golden amphora from the Siloam pool and sprinkled it on the south-west corner of the altar for burnt sacrifices, imploring plentiful rain for the next harvest (Is 12:3; PT Sukk 55b). According to this text, the separating of men and women in the temple is based on Zechariah (12:11-14): «In that day shall there be a great mourning in Jerusalem, as the mourning of Hadadrimmon in the valley of Megiddo. And the land shall mourn, every family apart; the family of the house of David apart, and their wives apart; and the family of the house of Levi apart, and their wives apart; the family of Shimei apart, and their wives apart; all the families that remain, every family apart, and their wives apart.» The mourning, men and women apart, according to some, refers to the Messiah, and to unworthy intention according to others (PT Sukk 55b) and so the separation of men and women.

In relation to the separation of men and women in the synagogues, the remains of the synagogues in Galilee, of Hellenistic style and basilica type, provide evidence of the existence of balconies probably to be used by women. However, in the synagogue at Dura Europos in Babylonia, which is not a basilica type, no remains of balconies have been found, a fact which, for some, reflects a more liberal attitude on the part of earlier rabbinical authorities towards women's participation in synagogue worship with men, but separated from them in a specially reserved place in the synagogue; for others, the silence of ancient rabbinical sources with respect to the separation of sexes proves that in these circles women were excluded from active participation in public worship, so nothing is regulated in this sense. On the few occasions when women had access to the synagogue a screen was set up to separate them from the men.

The fact that balconies existed in synagogues of Hellenistic stamp can point to the important role played by women in Hellenistic Jewish communities, a role which is reflected in the book of Acts (16:13-15): «And on the Sabbath we went out of the city by a river side, where prayer was wont to be made; and we sat down, and spake unto the women which resorted thither. And a certain woman named Lydia, seller of purple, of the city of Thyatira, which

71

worshipped God, heard us: whose heart the Lord opened, that she attended unto the things which were spoken of Paul. And when she was baptized, and her household, she besought us, saying: "If ye have judged me to be faithful to the Lord, come into my house, and abide there". And she constrained us.» Lydia's presence in the Jewish place of prayer is witness to women's participation in the Philippi community on the Sabbath.

It is possible that synagogues of basilica type, which had adopted architectural patterns from the temple at Jerusalem, followed the example of a courtyard for women in the aforesaid temple to separate the sexes, and this was done by building balconies. Synagogues that did not follow the basilica style would have taken special measures to separate women from men, placing them in a room adjoining the synagogue as appears to be the case in the synagogue at Dura Europos. This room communicated with the synagogue by a small window or a latticed opening.

To all events, the question remains open awaiting more convincing evidence; what is fact is that the separation of men and women became the rule in later synagogue worship.

3. NON-JEWS

As in the Jerusalem temple, where there existed a gentiles' courtyard, the synagogue also had followers (God fearers; gr. *foboumenoi ton theon*) or proselytes (etymologically, «those who come close to») among non-Jews. Paul's journeys prove this point. In Antioch in Pisidia, Paul speaks in the synagogue to the Israelites and God fearers (*foboumenoi ton theon:* Acts 13:14-16); «many of the Jews and religious proselytes (gr. *polloi... tôn sebomenôn prosêlytôn*) followed Paul and Barnabas...» (Acts 13:42-43). In Iconium, Paul and his companions they went both together into the synagogue of the Jews, and so spake, that a great multitude both of the Jews and also of the Greeks believed (Acts 14:1); in Thessalonica, after preaching in the synagogue of «the Jews», «some of them believed, and consorted with Paul and Silas; and of the devout Greeks (gr. *sebomenôn hellênôn*) a great multitude, and of the chief women not a few» (Acts 17:4); in Athens Paul «disputed in the synagogue with the Jews and devout persons (gr. *tois sebomenois*)» (Acts 17:17).

The midrašim testify to the presence of non-Jews in the synagogue, supporting this with biblical texts. The Song of Songs 1:15 («Behold thou art fair, my love; behold thou art fair; Thou hast doves' eyes») is explained as follows: «there is a type of dove which is used as a decoy, and its fellows are lured by its fragrance to its nest. In the same way, when a wise man (decoy bird) sits down to explain the doctrine, many strangers become proselytes» (*Cant Rabba* to 1,15; cf. also *Eccl Rabba* 5 and its parallel in *Midraš Tanḥuma* to Ex 18, p.69).

CHAPTER V

SYNAGOGUE WORSHIP

During the period in the desert and in Palestine, sacrificial cult depended entirely on the priests. The role of laymen and people was to present gifts to the priests who would offer them to Yahweh. Only priests could approach the altar and conduct liturgical rites. Also, priestdom was hereditary and limited to the descendants of Aaron's family.

In the synagogue, unlike the temple, the community was responsible for cult; if a priest were present, he took the same role as the rest of the congregation, although the final blessing was reserved for him. If no priest were present in the congregation, this blessing would not be given, instead, the *hazzan* recited its words. Synagogue cult is not sacrificial and it revolves round prayer and meditation on the sacred books.

According to Jewish law, ten Jewish male adults (13 years of age or more) make up a community (*'edah* or *minyan* [número]) and from the moment a *minyan* meets for prayer, public cult is celebrated. The Mishna establishes: «...The ark shall not be passed, hands shall not be raised (in blessing), the Torah shall not be read, nor the final part of the Prophets, the pause shall not be made nor the meeting (at funerals), nor shall the blessing be given to people in mourning, nor consolation, nor couples blessed, nor shall the blessing be given at meals, if it is not in the name of ten at least. To redeem property, nine plus the priest are enough; and the same to redeem a man (who has been consecrated)» (M Meg 4,2).

The fixed parts of synagogue worship are prayer and Scripture reading, probably followed by a homily. The oldest Jewish book of prayer still conserved is the «Seder 'Amram Gaon», from the ninth century.

The Sabbath and feast days

At the beginning of our times people went to the synagogue on the Sabbath and precept days; precisely one of the names for the synagogue was *sabbateion*. The evangelists often speak of Jesus intervening in the synagogues at Galilee. The texts do not always indicate the exact day of the week, but when they do so, it is invariably the Sabbath. Philo says that his doctors went to the synagogue or holy place only once a week (*De Vita Con.* 30-32), and Josephus refers to people meeting in the great synagogue at Tiberias on the Sabbath (*Vita* 276-279). However, the custom of meeting on the Sabbath eve had not yet been introduced, but they met from dawn on the Sabbath day; the most devote even came before sunrise to pray the *Šema'*. One text from the Mishna says: «At what time of morning should the *Šema'* be recited? From the moment one can distinguish between blue and white; R. Eleazar says: "from the moment blue can be distinguished from green; and it should be completed before the sun rises". R. Joshua said: "at three o'clock, because kings and princes rise at three. Whoever recites it later does not lose all merit, but it is worth the same as the reading of the Torah"» (M Ber 1,2). The synagogue service was very long and lasted till lunch, till midday.

Mondays and Thursdays

On Mondays and Thursdays, the people from the villages went to the city to do their shopping. They also made the most of this occasion to go to the law-courts. As there were no synagogues in the villages, it became the custom to meet on those days in the city synagogue for Scripture reading.

Mondays and Thursdays were observed in certain Jewish circles as days of fasting; the evangelists refer to the Pharisees' practice of fasting

76

(Mt 9:14; Mk 2:18-20; Lk 5:33-35). The *Tosefta'* reads: «The second and fifth days, individuals took part in community fasting. On those days there were tribunals in the towns; the synagogues were entered and readings were made, this was not done during private fasting» (Ta'an 2,4). When the community fasts it is forbidden to eat, drink, bathe and anoint oneself, wear sandals, make use of a bed, work; the synagogue is entered to recite twenty four blessings, the priests raise their hands four times a day: none of this is done in private fasting... (cf. PT Pes 30c; Sof 21).

This custom of reading the Scriptures on Mondays and Thursdays — which some *Tannaim* claim goes back to the times of the prophets and elders, and others to Ezra — existed before the year 70 of our era.

1. THE TWO BLESSINGS, THE ŠEMA' AND THE COMMANDMENTS

According to the Mishna, morning synagogue service began on the Sabbath with the chanting of the *Šema'* or declaration of faith by Israel's people, preceded by two blessings (Heb. *běrakot*) and followed by another; at evening service, the *Šema'* was preceded and followed by two blessings (M Ber 1,4).

It is called *Šema'* as Dt 6:4-9, the first of the Bible texts that make up the prayer, begins with this word.

The two blessings

The text of the two blessings was substantially as follows:

1. Blessed be the Lord, king of the world, who made the light and created the darkness; who made peace and created everything; with thy mercy illuminated the earth and its inhabitants; and with thy goodness reneweth the works of creation day by day. Blessed be the Lord, our God, for the glory of the works of thy hands and for the light giver of light thou hast made for thy praise. *Selah! Blessed be the Lord our God, who has made the stars.*
2. Thou hast loved us without measure, our Lord God, and with immense mercy hath taken mercy on us, our Father and King. For our

brethren who have faith in thee, and to whom thou taught the precepts of life, have mercy on us and teach us. Direct our eyes towards thy commandments; unite our hearts to love and fear thy name, and we shall not be ashamed for ever. For thou art the God our Saviour, who has chosen us among all nations and tongues, and has placed us confidently near thy Great Name — *Selah* — that we lovingly praise thee and only thee. *Blessed be the Lord who has chosen with love His people Israel.*

After these two blessings came the *Šemaʿ*.

The Šemaʿ

The *Šemaʿ* is composed of the three passages from the Pentateuch: Dt 6:4-9; Dt 11:13-21 and Nm 15:37-41, with the latter probably being a later addition. In these passages the oneness of God and His close union with His people is affirmed at the same time as constant remembrance of Him is ordered.

These three passages are named in the Mishna after the words they commence with: *Šemaʿ* (Dt 6:4), *Wĕ-hayah ʾim šamoaʿ* (Dt 11:13-21) and *Wa-yomer* (Nm 15:37-41). Here are the texts:

I. *Hear (Heb.* Šemaʿ), *O Israel: The Lord our God is one Lord: and thou shalt love the Lord thy God with all thine heart, and with all thy soul, and with all thy might. And these words, which I command thee this day, shall be in thine heart: and thou shalt teach them diligently unto thy children, and shalt talk of them when thou sittest in thine house, and when thou walkest by the way, and when thou liest down, and when thou risest up. And thou shalt bind them for a sign upon thine hand, and they shall be as frontlets between thine eyes. And thou shalt write them upon the posts of thy house, and on thy gates* (Dt 6:4-9).

II. *If ye shall hearken (Heb.* Wĕ-hayah ʾim šamoaʿ) *diligently unto my commandments which I command you this day, to love the Lord your God, and to serve him with all your heart and with all your soul, that I will give you the rain of your land in due season, the first rain and the latter rain, that thou mayest gather in thy corn, and thy wine, and thine oil. And I will send grass in thy fields for thy cattle, that thou mayest eat and be full.*

Take heed to yourselves, that your heart be not deceived, and ye turn aside, and serve other gods, and worship them; and then the Lord's wrath be kindled against you, and he shut up the heaven, that there be no rain, and that the land yield not her fruit; and lest ye perish quickly from off the good land which the Lord giveth you.

Therefore shall ye lay up these my words in your heart and in your soul, and bind them for a sign upon thy hand, that they may be as frontlets between your eyes. And ye shall teach them your children, speaking of them when thou sittest in thine house, and when thou walkest by the way, when thou liest down, and when thou risest up. And thou shalt write them upon the door posts of thine house, and upon thy gates: that your days may be multiplied, and the days of your children, in the land which the Lord sware unto your fathers to give them, as the days of heaven upon the earth (Dt 11:13-21).

III.   *And the Lord (Heb.* Wa-yomer) *spake unto Moses, saying, Speak unto the children of Israel, and bid them that they make fringes in the borders of their garments throughout their generations, and that they put upon the fringe of the borders a ribband of blue: and it shall be unto you for a fringe, that ye may look upon it, and remember all the commandments of the Lord, and do them; and that ye seek not after your own heart and your own eyes, after which ye use to go a whoring: that ye may remember, and do all my commandments, and be holy unto your God. I am the Lord your God, which brought you out of the land of Egypt, to be your God: I am the Lord your God* (Nm 15:37-41).

The first of these texts, Dt 6:4-9, speaks of the obligation of always keeping the Holy commandments; the second, Dt 11:13-21, of rewards for those who keep them, chastisement for offenders and the duty of keeping them and teaching them to the young; the third, Nm 15:37-41, interpreted literally, gave rise to the custom of carrying phylacteries.

Phylacteries are small boxes containing written verses from the Bible and were tied to one's forehead and arms (Mt 23:5).

The commandments

Originally the commandments formed a part of the *Šema'*
(M Tam 5,1) and it seems that there existed Hebrew manuscripts
in circulation that contained only the commandments and the *Šema'*. An example of these is the Naš Papyrus with the text of the
ten commandments and Dt 6:4-6. Later the text was eliminated
from the ten commandments.

> The Naš Papyrus dates from the Maccabees period, between 165
> and 37 B.C.

The order in which these texts from the *Šema'* were recited is
a point under discussion. According to R. Joshua ben Karha (140-
165 A.D.) Dt 6 is recited first, then Dt 11 and finally Nm 15
(M Ber 2,2).

The *Šema'* began by being recited privately: «in thine house,
and when thou walkest by the way, when thou liest down, and
when thou risest up» (Dt 11:19-20; cf. *Letter of Aristeas* 160; Josephus, *Ant.* 4,213; M Ber 1,3), although already, from ancient times,
it passed to public recitation when the community met for morning
service (M Tam 5,1; M Meg 4,3; M Pes 4,8). It was recited as an
anthem between the officiator and the congregation. In this public
recitation, after *Hear, Israel* the verse «Blessed be the Lord, whose
glory lasts for ever» was introduced.

The *Šema'* was recited twice every day, in the morning and in
the evening, and all male adult Israelites were obliged to do so
(M Ber 1,1-4); children, women and slaves were exempted (M Ber
3,3); it could be recited in the vernacular language (M Sot 7,1; Sot
7,7; BT Sot 32b; Ber 13a). According to the Mishna, the *Šema'* is
recited in the evening from the time the priests come back to eat
their oblations until the first fast: this was R. Eleazar's feeling. «The
elders said: "until midnight".» R. Gamaliel said: «"until dawn".
On one occasion, his sons, returning from a feast, told him: "we
have not recited the *Šema'*"; he replied: "as dawn has not yet come,
you are obliged to recite it"» (M Zer 1,1).

As the Mishna refers to the fact that the *Šema'* was recited by
the priests in the temple, we may assume that it was in use prior

to the year 70 of our times. Indeed, Flavius Josephus considers it as being very old when he states it was established by Moses himself (*Ant.* 4,8,13 [212]).

2. THE «TĚFILLAH» OR THE PRAYER ITSELF

After the *Šema'* came the prayer itself, the *Těfillah*. A talmudical source (BT Ber 26b) says that prayer in the synagogue corresponds to sacrificial worship in the temple; even in the period when the synagogue and the temple co-existed, prayers were celebrated in the synagogue at the same time as the sacrifices in the temple; after the destruction of the temple, synagogue prayer became a substitute for sacrifices.

The Eighteen Blessings (Šěmoneh 'Eśreh)

Jewish prayer, in Second Temple times, was called blessing, as it often commenced and terminated with the formula «Blessed be the Lord» and others of a similar nature. From the Talmud we know the text of the Eighteen Blessings (*Šěmoneh 'Eśreh*) which made up the *Těfillah,* although elements are included that do not always date back to the first century; in spite of being of a later date than the *Šema'*, the text of the Eighteen Blessings is very old; some are later than the year 70 of our times (date of the destruction of the temple at Jerusalem by Tito's legions), as they presume the fall of the city and the interruption of sacrificial cult. Different versions of the Eighteen Blessings have been conserved, so it may be that in the first century there was only a guide to prayer rather than a fixed text.

The *Šěmoneh 'Eśreh* prayer was so important that it was considered the prayer par excellence and was given the name *ha-těfillah,* «the prayer». In its latest form, the Babylonian version, there are nineteen blessings instead of eighteen, as one was added — the twelfth — against «informers, ... those that do evil and ... the insolent» (which appears to be a reference to Christians). Even though they totaled nineteen, this set of blessings continued being called *Šěmoneh 'Eśreh* (lit. Eighteen Blessings).

The *Šĕmoneh 'Eśreh* are the main prayers that every Jew should recite three times a day; in the morning, in the first hour of the afternoon (when offering is made [Heb. *minḥah]* in the temple) and at sunset (M Ber 3,3; 4,1).

The blessings were said by the person who led the service and those attending joined in answering «Amen».

The officiator could adapt these blessings at his will in such a way that the prayer was especially prolonged to celebrate the New Year, the Day of Purification or days of public fasting (M R.H. 4,6; Tos R.H. 4,6-7; M Ta'an 2,2-5). However, both the opening and the conclusion of this prayer soon took on a fixed formula.

The context of the eighteen blessings refers to needs of daily life and people's desire for Messianic restoration. It began with praise to God (Nos. 1-3) and concluded with an act of thanksgiving for his goodness, asking for his blessing in general (18-19); the fourth to the ninth ask for knowledge, regret, pardon, freedom from evil, health and fruits of the earth; from the tenth to the sixteenth, the reuniting of the dispersed, the restoration of national sovereignty, the destruction of the impious, reward for the just, the reconstruction of Jerusalem, the coming of the Messiah, that the prayers be heard and sacrificial cult restored. The feelings expressed in these blessings are to be found throughout the Palestinian Targum to the Pentateuch and other liturgical paraphrases in the O.T.

Here is the text of the Babylonian version, the most recent and extensive:

1. Blessed art thou, Lord our God and God of our fathers, God of Abraham, God of Isaac and God of Jacob, great, mighty and fearful God, most high God, who bestowed abundant grace and createst all things and rememberest the promises of grace to the fathers and bringest a Redeemer to their children's children for thy Name's sake out of love. O King, who bringest help and salvation and who art a shield. *Blessed art thou, Lord, shield of Abraham.*

2. Lord, thou art almighty for ever, who makest the dead alive. Thou art mighty to help, thou who sustainest the living out of grace, makest the dead alive out of great mercy, supportest those who fall, healest the sick, freest the captive, and keepest thy word faithfully to them who sleep in the dust. And who is like thee, Lord

82

of mighty deeds, and who is comparable to thee, King, who makest dead and alive and causest help to spring forth. And thou art faithfull to make the dead alive. *Blessed art thou, Lord, who makest the dead alive.*

3. Thou art holy and thy Name is holy and the holy praise thee every day. Blessed art thou, Lord, holy, God.

4. Thou grantest knowledge to mankind and teachest men understanding. Grant us the knowledge, understanding and discernment (which come) from thee. *Blessed art thou, Lord, who grantest knowledge.*

5. Lead us back, our Father, to thy Torah; and bring us, our King, to thy service, and cause us to return in perfect repentance to thy presence. *Blessed art thou, Lord, who delightest in repentance.*

6. Forgive us, our Father, for we have sinned; pardon us, our King, for we have transgressed. For thou forgivest and pardonest. *Blessed art thou, Lord, gracious, rich in forgiveness.*

7. Look on our affliction and plead our cause, and redeem us speedily for thy Name's sake; for thou art a mighty redeemer. *Blessed art thou, Lord, redeemer of Israel.*

8. Heal us, O Lord, and we shall be healed, save us and we shall be saved; for thou art our praise. And bring perfect healing to all our wounds. For thou art a God and King who heals, faithfull and merciful. *Blessed art thou, Lord, who healest the sick of thy people Israel.*

9. Bless this year us, Lord our God, and cause all its produce to prosper; and bless the land; and satisfy us with goodness; and bless our year as the good years. *Blessed art thou, Lord, who blessest the years.*

10. Proclaim our liberation with the great trumpet, and raise a banner to gather together our dispersed, and assemble us from the four corners of the earth. *Blessed art thou, Lord, who gatherest the banished of thy people Israel.*

11. Restore our judges as in former times and our counsellors as in the beginning; and take from us sorrow and sighing; and reign over us, thou Lord alone, in grace and mercy; and justify us in judgement; *Blessed art thou, Lord, King, who lovest justice and judgement.*

12. And for informers let there be no hope; and let all who

do wickedness quickly perish; and let them all be speedily destroyed; and uproot and crush and hurl down and humble the insolent, speedily in our days. *Blessed art thou, Lord, who crushest enemies and humblest the insolent.*

13. Over righteous and over the pious; and over the elders of thy people of the house of Israel; and over the remnant of their Torah scholars; and over the righteous proselytes; and over us, may thy mercy shower down, Lord our God. And give a rich reward to all who faithfully trust in thy Name. And cause our portion to be with them for ever, that we may not be put to shame. For we have trusted in thee. *Blessed art thou, Lord, support and trust of the righteous.*

14. And to Jerusalem, thy city, return with mercy and dwell in its midst as thou hast spoken; and build it soon in our days to be an everlasting building; and raise up quickly in its midst the throne of David. *Blessed art thou, Lord, who buildest Jerusalem.*

15. Cause the shoot of David to shoot forth quickly, and raise up his horn bay thy salvation. For we wait on thy salvation all the day. *Blessed art thou, Lord, who causest the horn of salvation to shoot forth.*

16. Hear our voice, Lord our God; spare us and have mercy on us, and accept our prayer with mercy and pleasure; For thou art a God who hearest prayers and supplications; and let us not return empty, our King, from before thy Face. For thou hearest the prayer of thy people Israel with mercy. *Blessed art thou, Lord, who hearest prayer.*

17. Be pleased, Lord our God, with thy people Israel and with their prayer. Bring back the worship into the Holy of Holies of thy house and accept in love and pleasure the sacrifices of Israel and her prayer. And may the worship offered by Israel thy people be pleasing to thee always. O that our eyes might see thy return with mercy to Zion. *Blessed art thou, Lord, who causest thy presence* (Šĕkinah) *to return to Zion.*

18. We praise thee, for thou art the Lord our God and the God of our fathers for ever and ever, the rock of our life, the shield of our salvation from generation to generation. We praise thee and recount thy praise, for our life that is given into thy hand and for our souls which are in thy charge; and for thy wonders to us every

day; and for thy marvels; and for thy deeds of goodness at every time, at evening and morning and midday. All-Good, of whose mercy there is no end, Merciful One, whose grace increases, we wait on thee forever. And for all this be praised and thy Name be exalted, our King, forever in all eternity. And may all that lives praise thee, selah, and praise thy Name in truth, thou God, our salvation and our help, *selah. Blessed art thou, Lord, All-Good is thy Name, and it is fitting to praise thee.*

19. Bring peace, goodness and blessing, grace and favour and mercy over us and over all Israel, thy people. Bless us our Father, all of us together, with the light of thy Face. For by the light of thy Face thou hast given us Lord our God, the Torah of life and loving kindness and righteousness and blessing and mercy and life and peace. And may it be good in thine eyes to bless thy people Israel at all times and in every hour with thy peace. *Blessed art thou, Lord, who blessed thy people Israel with peace. Amen* (Schürer, *Historia* II, 590).

> In the Palestinian version the text of the *Šĕmoneh 'Eśreh* has only eighteen blessings which are sometimes shorter, but the structure as a whole is almost exactly the same. Perhaps the most important variation in the Palestinian version is the absence of one blessing in particular — the fifteenth in the Babylonian text— imploring the coming of the Messiah; its content is expressed briefly in the fourteenth blessing. In particular, the doxologies that finalize each of the blessings correspond almost entirely to those of the Babylonian version, demonstrating the framework within which it originated, that is, during the last three decades of the first century of our era. The text of the Palestinian version is probably the original and earlier.

It is a well known argument among rabbis whether the whole of the blessings text must be read or if a summary of them can be recited. According to Rabbi Gamaliel II the complete eighteen blessings should be recited; according to R. Joshua, only a summary; R. Aqiba's opinion is that if the prayer flows rapidly through the lips of the person praying, he will recite the eighteen; if not, a summary (M Ber 4,3). From this discussion it is clear that the structure of the blessings was fixed, but the text fluctuated (longer or shorter according to the circumstances).

S. Pekoli set out the order of the eighteen blessings in Yabne, in Rabbi Gamaliel's presence.

Many are the traditions that date the order of the blessings back to the earliest times of the second temple, 536ff B.C. (BT Meg 18a; BT Ber 33a; Sifre Dt 343, p.395). An echo of these blessings is to be found in Ecclesiastes 51; many of the acts of thanksgiving and of the prayers in this chapter are similar to the final part of the eighteen blessings, although there is quite a difference between both texts. There are also points of contact between Ecclesiastes 36,1-17 and the blessings the High Priest gave after the Scripture readings on Expiation Day (M Yom 7,1). Parallels to the prayers in the Eighteen blessings can be found in Solomon's Psalms.

The Mishna (Tam 5,1) gives a list of the blessings that should be recited with the *Šema'* and of the distribution of the Eighteen Blessings the priest must recite at intervals during the morning sacrificial offering; it also records a series of eight blessings the High Priest recites after the reading on the Day of Expiation (M R.H. 4,11). The king also recited the blessings on the tabernacle feast, but only once every seven years (M Yom 7,1; Sot 7,7). The content of these blessings and their pattern can be found in the Mishna (Yom 4,18) and in the Palestinian Talmud (PT Yom 44b). These blessings are very similar to the ones quoted in the Soferim tractate (13,7-14), still in use today.

3. SCRIPTURE READING

The reading of the Scriptures followed the *Tĕfillah,* and was accompanied in Palestine by an Aramaean version. Scripture reading was the centre of Synagogue worship at the beginning of our times, and this is testified by the New Testament and by Philo and Flavius Josephus. The Mishna gives further confirmation with the inclusion of subjects relating to the synagogue in the *Mĕgillah* treatise, which revolves round Scripture reading in the synagogue. The Scriptures were read on the Sabbath, on precept days and those of public fasting.

The Torah

The reading of the Scriptures, and of the Torah and the Pentateuch in particular, is in all probability as old as the synagogue itself. According to pre-Christian Jewish sources, it was Moses who ordered the reading of the Law on the Sabbath, on feast days, new moon and days between feasts, while Ezra ordered it to be done on market days too (Mondays and Thursdays) and at evening service — *minhah* — on the Sabbath (PT Meg 75a).

While prayer could also be said in private, Scripture reading was only done in public and in the synagogue. According to the Mishna «if fewer than ten are present... neither the Torah can be read nor the final part of the Prophets...» (M Meg 4,3).

In New Testament times the Law or Torah (the first five books of the Pentateuch) was read, followed by the Prophets. The earliest rabbinical sources only mention the reading of the Torah, but from the New Testament (Lk 4:17 and Acts 13:15) it can clearly be deduced that the reading of the Prophets was common practice at the beginning of our times at the synagogues in Palestine and in the Diaspore. The texts quoted refer respectively to reading in the synagogues at Nazareth and Antioch in Pisidia.

The reading of the Prophets was called *Haftarah* (conclusion or end of the Torah reading), an expression that referred to the order in which the Prophets were read during synagogue liturgy (BT Ned 40a). The Torah finalized with the Prophets and was completed by them, according to Hebrew expressions in use such as *hiftir bĕ-nabiʿ*: dismiss (the community) with the Prophets (PT Sanh 1,19a), from which *Haftarah* also means dismissal reading, as after the reading of the Prophets, followed by the giving of blessings, synagogue service came to an end (Ber 4,7). The reader of the Prophets was called *maftir bĕ-nabiʿ*.

The reading of the Prophets was done by a single person, who also read, or perhaps simply repeated, the final part of the reading of the Torah, although this detail is only reflected in later documents (BT Meg 23a; PT Meg 4,75c). The Prophets were not read consecutively, there was a kind of anthology or a passage was selected each week (cf Lk 4:16ff). At least, this seems to be deduced from the Mishna (Meg 3,4.6; 4,4) where it is established that the reader may leave out verses from the Prophets but not from the Law. This same tractate makes several references to the reading of the Law «in the set order» but never refers to any order established for the *Haftarah*. The *Tosefta'* determines some of the Prophets' readings for certain days (Tos Meg 4,1). As from the year 300 in Palestine (BT Meg 30b) and at the beginning of the fourth century an order for the readings of the Prophets is mentioned (BT Git 60a).

The reader or readers

Any male over twelve years of age could read the Scriptures (M Meg 4,6); if a levite or priest were present they took preference for the readings (Git 5,8). Women could not read (Tos Meg 4,11). There was no permanent reader; sometimes one of the congregation was invited to read. It was the custom to stand while reading (BT Yom 7,1; Sot 7,7; cf Lk 4:16).

At the beginning, the custom was to have various readers; on Mondays, Thursdays and Sabbath evenings there were three (M Meg 4,1); five on feast days; six on Expiation Day and seven on Sabbath mornings (Tos Meg 4,11). On Sabbath evenings the Prophets were not read, nor on Mondays, Thursdays, new-moon and days between feasts (M Meg 4,1-2).

Should there be only one qualified reader present in the synagogue, he would read the Torah pausing after each part of the text (Tos Meg 4,12). The Palestinian Talmud says that Jews living in the Hellenistic world did not share the custom of calling three, five or seven readers but just one. Philo confirms this point indicating that the same person read the Pentateuch on the Sabbath (Philo in Eusebius, *Praeparatio Evangelica* VIII, 7,13), although this was not the practice everywhere, as in the diaspore, sometimes, when there was only one reader who knew Hebrew, he began the reading and completed it, while another read the texts in the vernacular language (Meg 4,13), the vernacular being the version of the LXX or the Greek version of Aquila (from the second century of our era).

The reader was invited by the head of the synagogue or by the *hazzan;* each person who read did so invited by others; while the *hazzan* read, another, standing, took his place (Tos Meg 4,21).

It was only after the Talmud period that the figure of the Scripture reader was institutionalized and it became a job for specialists. The Mishna establishes readings for the four sabbaths preceding the Easter feast (M Meg 3,4). Each of these readings was known by the word it commenced with: *Šĕkalim* (Ex 30:11-16), *Zakor* (Dt 25:17-19), *Parah* (Nm 19:1-21) and *Ha-hodeš* (Ex 12: 1-20). Special readings were made on other feasts (M Meg 3,5ff).

Order of the readings

For the rest of the days and ordinary sabbaths there was no fixed order for the readings. R. Meir and R. Judah, in their different ways, proposed a continuous reading of the Law. The Palestinian cycle of three years' reading of the Pentateuch is mentioned in the Babylonian Talmud and was established in the third century, although it could well have been the custom prior to that time. The Pentateuch was divided into 155 parts (Heb. *sĕdarim),* one for every Sabbath, so every three years the whole of the Torah was read.

At the beginning there was a certain amount of flexibility to choose the passage to be read, although on feast days texts relating to the feast in question were usually chosen. The list of paragraphs for reading on each Sabbath took some time to become fixed. The text of the Prophets was chosen to correspond with the Torah text, but the determination of the Prophets' texts for synagogue readings came later than that of the Torah texts.

Translation or «targum»

The Scriptures were read in Hebrew; they were not recited from memory to avoid the risk of forgetting or altering the tiniest part (PT Meg 74d). But Hebrew was no longer the language spoken by the people, it was now Aramaean — giving rise to a situation that can be compared with Latin in the Catholic liturgy a few years ago. In order to allow the congregation to understand the contents of the text, the reader had to pause to allow the translator to give an Aramaean version (*targum*) of what had been read in Hebrew.

Targum is an Aramaean word that means translation and refers to the Aramaean version of the Bible that had been read in the synagogues since before the Christian era.

The Mishna has preserved precise rules on how to do this: «The person who reads the Law shall not read less than three verses. For the translator he shall not read more than one verse at a time, but he shall read three of the Prophets; if three verses are from three different parts he shall not read more than one at a time. In the reading of the Prophets he may jump from one text to another (Heb. *mĕdallĕgin bĕ-nabi'*), but not in the Torah. How much can he jump? Not too much so the translator does not have to pause» (M Meg 4,4; PT Meg 75b). From this quotation from the Mishna we can see that the Law (the Pentateuch) is translated verse by verse, while the translation of the Prophets was usually three verses at a time. The Mishna (Meg 4,19) establishes that (in the twelve minor prophets) the reader can jump from one prophet to another; the only restriction is not to jump from the end of the book to the beginning.

Although the reading of the Prophets was not a universal custom, it can be said that they were read after the long Torah reading on fasting days, Sabbath mornings and feast days, but not on Mondays, Thursdays or Sabbath evenings after the short Torah reading (BT Šab 24a). Later Talmudical sources indicate that on feast days the scrolls (*mĕgillot*) were read: the Song (at Easter), Ruth (at Pentecost), Lamentations (the nine days of *Av*), Ecclesiastes (at Tabernacles), Esther (at *Purim*), with the reading of Esther as the custom that goes back further in time (M Meg cc. 1-2).

The translation of the Torah reading was done more meticulously than that of the Prophets; while the former was translated one verse at a time, the Prophets could be translated three verses at a time; on occasions an approximate translation of the Prophets' passage was given and on others it was not even translated (M Meg 4,4; BT Meg 23b).

There is a difference of opinion over whether the Prophets were read before or after the sermon. C. W. Bacher (*Die Exegetische,* 14) says they concluded the service. To the contrary Elbogen (*Gottesdienst,* 175) observes that there is no evidence that the service closed with the reading of the Prophets and he argues that *hiftir bĕ-naḇi'* (Meg 4,1-5) does not mean «dismiss the congregation with the Prophets» but «finalize the Scripture reading with the Prophets».

The translation was usually into Aramaean; sometimes into Greek or other vernacular languages. The Talmud mentions Coptic, Elamite and Madianite, but if there is simply a reference to translation it means into Aramaean (M Meg 2,1; BT Šab 115a).

The translator

The person who translated the Scriptures into Aramaean was called *mĕturgĕman,* derived from the Hebrew root *tirgem* (translate, clarify).

> *Mĕturgĕman* is a translation of a holy text (the Bible) in a holy place (the synagogue) with the catechetic intention of illustrating God's people (the community) and exhorting them according to the meaning of the words of the Law and the Prophets (following the liturgical cycles of readings), in the same way they were explained and understood in Israel's tradition (in the *pesat* sense: that is, not merely a literal sense but the commonly accepted one, as a Babylonian Talmudical texts says: that sense which even the sadducees agree on (BT San 33b). The *mĕturgĕman* uses a series of technical resorts in translation that today might seem fanciful and arbitrary, but that are completely justified and accepted by the hermeneutics of those times and by the subjacent theology (M. Pérez, *Targum y Midrás,* 102).

This translation of the Holy Scriptures could be done by anyone who knew Hebrew, even if he were under age (M Meg 4,6); the latter were only excluded from the reading of the book of Esther at the *Purim* feast: everyone is qualified to read the *Mĕgillah* except the deaf, the idiot and children, although R. Judah also admitted children (BT Meg 2,4).

No qualification was needed for translating, although a certain hierarchy between reader and translator should be observed: the disciple translated the scholar and an inferior translated his superior (Tos Meg 4,21).

The Aramaean language at the beginning of our era

To understand the *Targum's* origins it is necessary first of all to consider the evolution of the Aramaean language and its use in Jesus' times. As we have just said, in Palestine at the beginning of our times Aramaean was spoken, although in some areas Hebrew was still used, in its later Mishnaic form.

> With reference to the types of Aramaean in the first century we must consider the differences between Palestinian Aramaean as it appears in the Palestinian Targums, the Palestinian Talmud and the Palestinian Midrašim, which distinguish it from the Aramaean in the O.T., the Qumran, the Muraba'at and the Onkelos and the Babylonian Targum to the Prophets; the Aramaean closest to that spoken in Palestine, or at least part of Palestine, is the one found in the Palestinian Targum to the Pentateuch. But the question of different types of Aramaean is still open.

Rules for translation

The Mishna gives detailed rules for the translating of the Scriptures in the Synagogue:

The reader reads the passage in Hebrew and this is immediately translated into Aramaean by the *mĕturgĕman* who stands beside the reader. Each reader of the Law must read at least three verses, which are translated. The same with the Prophets. If a verse makes sense on its own, it is read and then translated. The Law must be read in its complete form and nothing omitted; verses from the Prophets may be eliminated. The translation must be simultaneous and oral (M Meg 4,1; BT Meg 74d) without the written translated text to hand, as this could be confused with the inspired Word. The Babylonian Talmud gives another reason: the difference between the holy text and its translation and interpretation must be made clear in people's minds (BT Meg 32a). This difference is understood by Jesus' disciples in the Gospels which distinguish clearly between the Scriptures' words on Ely and the interpretation of them by the Scribes (Mt 17:10; Mk 9:11). The Law or Torah should be read because it is unchangeable and must be kept unaltered, sacred, as God's Word, but no translation, not even the closest, can reach the category of the Holy Word; this is why it cannot be fixed in writing. Privately and in preparation for synagogue service, these translated texts can be used. There is no reference to translations being read from a written targum until the fourth century of our era (PT Meg 74d).

The golden rule for translating a text is expressed by R. Judah ben Ilai in these terms: «He who translates literally is a falsifier; he who adds something is a blasphemer» (Tos Meg 4,41; BT Qid 49a). The translation of Ex 24:10 illustrates this principle. Ex 24:10 reads: «They saw the God of Israel». Translated literally would mean lying, as nobody can say he has seen God. Substituting «angel» for «God» would be blasphemous, as a creature would be substituted for the creator. The appropriate translation according to R. Judah is: *They saw* the glory of the *God of Israel.* The spirit that inspires this translation can be seen in Jn 12:41 where it says that Esaias saw his (Christ's) glory (cf. Is 6:15).

So the sense of the *mĕturgĕman*'s translation should not be literal; its aim was to enable people to understand the meaning of the text; it was more paraphrastic and homiletic, a real actualization of the biblical text. Therefore an academic version is not entailed but a liturgical-kerigmatical-catechetical activity. A *mĕturgĕman* is a preacher rather than a philologist and is as attentive to the text he is translating as to the public he translates for.

According to the *Tosefta'* (Meg 4,31ff) there are passages in the Scriptures which are read and translated, others that are read but not translated and yet others that are neither read nor translated. Texts that could shock simple people are omitted or not translated. For example, the story of Reuben sleeping with Bilhah, his father's concubine (Gen 35:22) is read but not translated. We know that Rabbi Ananiah ben Gamaliel read in (the synagogue of) Cabul: «Reuben went and lay with Bilhah his father's concubine: and Israel heard it (and was greatly troubled). Now the sons of Jacob were twelve, and he told the translator: "translate only the last part"» (Tos Meg 4,31). Other texts that are read but not translated, according to M Meg 4,10 are: the second story of the Golden Calf (Ex 32); the story of Amnon and Tamar (2 Sam 13). The priests' blessing (Nm 6:24-26) and the story of David and

Bath-Sheba (2 Sam 11:2-17) are neither read nor translated and in other passages if there was an offensive expression, it could be substituted by another.

As continuous reading was not introduced suddenly, the Palestinian Targum must have taken shape gradually, so its texts may date from different periods.

Two cycles of readings

The Torah was read in two reading cycles of different lengths: one, the Babylonian, lasted one year; another, the Palestinian, lasted three. We do not know exactly if these reading cycles had been established by the beginning of our times. *Tannaitic* sources in the Mishna and the *baraitot* only mention the number of readers and the minimum number of verses that each must read or the total to be read between them all. The reading should be continuous, so each day the reading should continue where it left off the day before. However, in this respect there were two different opinions: one, Rabbi Meir's, that the Sabbath morning and evening, Mondays and Thursdays, the reading should carry on from the previous day; and that of R. Judah ben Ilai, R. Meir's contemporary, who maintained that only the Sabbath morning reading should be continuous, in such a way that each Sabbath the reading should continue from where it stopped the previous Sabbath (Tos Meg 4,10; Meg 31b). When the Mishna (Meg 3,6) speaks of the reading of the Law «according to the established order», it should be interpreted in the light of these two different points of view (Meg 3,6).

Continuous reading was suspended on certain feast days, immediately prior to or following feasts which had certain fixed readings. The Mishna indicates the precise reading for the four sabbaths in Adar (the month preceding Nisan), Easter, Pentecost, New Year, Day of Atonement, Tabernacles, Dedication, Lots, as well as other feast days, that is, the first days of the month (new moon), *ma'ǎma-dot* (synagogue services coinciding with the turns of levites and priests who did service in the temple) and fasting days (Meg 3,4-6). The readings set for the four sabbaths preceding the Nisan month were called by the initial Hebrew words Sekalim, Zakór, Parah and Hahodes. The choice of these texts for this month is clear: all of them speak of the obligation of paying temple taxes and of complying with Easter preparation...

That the Pentateuch should be read in continuous reading, in a certain order, seems to be a basic principle, but the concrete way of doing it was not determined, being left to each synagogue's judgment. This order or reading plan would take some time to become definitely fixed.

> Jews and Samaritans today complete the Pentateuch reading in a year's cycle, Babylonian Talmud style (Meg 29b), in contrast to the three yearly Palestinian cycle: those (Jews) from the East (i.e. Palestine) complete the Pentateuch reading in three years. The Babylonian cycle was in use in Palestine by the third century. The Palestinian cycle was in use until the yearly Babylonian cycle imposed itself. The Masoretic order of the Pentateuch in a hundred and four parts is probably due to this three year cycle. But there are also calculations for distribution in a hundred and sixty one, a hundred and sixty six and a hundred and seventy five parts (PT Šab 15c), which point perhaps to the existence of a three and a half year cycle (two complete readings of the Pentateuch in seven years).

4. THE SERMON

Following the Scripture reading came the sermon, mostly in Aramaean (Heb. *děrašah* or *děraša'*, derived from *daraš*, research, interpret, expound). The Hebrew name for preacher was *daršan* (Aram. *daroša'*). The sermon was common practice in Palestine and in the diaspore towards the middle of the first century of our times. Tradition dates this practice back to Moses (BT Meg 32a). It could be given by any educated Jew and consisted of an illustrative paraphrase of the texts read, with a large dose of quotations out of all context and consideration of historical order. In a way the sermon was an extension of the Targum or Scripture translation. It frequently centred on the Prophets (Lk 4:16ff). Normally, if there was a sage present in the synagogue, he would address the congregation; if none were present, anyone who had anything to say did so, if the head of the synagogue considered him appropriate. The Babylonian Talmud, setting out the daily order of public fasting, stipulates who should invite the congregation to repentance: «If an elder is present (a sanhedrin member), he should exhort to repentance, if not, a sage, and if there is no sage, any distinguished person» (BT Ta'an 16a). It was frequent to invite a visiting sage to give the sermon (Acts 13:14). To all events it is not sure that the reading of the Prophets was always followed by the sermon, as not all the synagogues had someone qualified to give it.

> The sermon is at the same time an exaltation and glorification of the Lord on High, a theological education given to all the people and an invitation to live according to the Law. At the beginning of our times, the scribes and the pharisees were the ones who most frequently addressed the people through the sermon, turning it into their best ally to spread their ideas and increase their influence over the people.

The sermon did not form part of the synagogue service itself, as it ended with the reading of the Prophets, as we have just said. But as one of the obligations of a good Jew was to study the Torah, the appropriate moment for it was considered to be the Sabbath, a day of rest, when the assembly was gathered. This practice is referred to twice in the New Testament (Lk 4:16-22 and Acts 13:15); *Tannaitic* and *Amoraitic* traditions also contain references to it.

The subject of the sermon centres on God's piety and holiness towards humanity and towards all men. In the Mishna, *Tosefta'* or any other source, no rules governing the sermon's subject or method are to be found and it enjoyed enormous freedom, varying according to the place, time and circumstances. The Jewish sermon, to all events, is a fine example of *Hagadic Midraš,* applying the biblical text to the present situation. In the N.T. these sermons consisted of explanations of how Bible texts were fulfilled in Jesus... In an earlier form, translation and sermon were probably combined; this form can be represented by the Targum to the Pentateuch, Pal Targ, which presents considerable licence in its paraphrases.

Santa María la Blanca synagogue (Toledo)

Tránsito synagogue (Toledo)

In Philo the sermon appears as almost the most important part of synagogue service. In his works he gives three brief descriptions of synagogue worship (cf. Eusebius, *Praep. Evang.* VIII, 7,12-13, taken from the first book of the Hypothetica; *De Spec. Leg.* 11,15 [62]; on the Essenes, *Quod omnis probus,* 12 [82]).

The post-Talmudical Soferim treatise (cc. 10-12) offers a series of detailed rules for synagogue worship.

5. THE *KADDIŠ*

The sermon ended with this sentence in Aramaean: «Blessed be thy name for ever and ever». In pre-Christian times this phrase was further developed, giving rise to a long prayer in Aramaean called *Kaddiš,* which was also said at other moments during the liturgy. The form of the prayer at the beginning of our era is not easy to define, but it must have been more or less as follows:

> «Exalted and hallowed be thy great name on the earth which He created with His will; and may thy kingdom come during thy lifetime and that of all the house of Israel, very soon.» ℞ «Amen.»
>
> «Blessed be thy great name, world without end. Blessed and praised, celebrated and exalted, extolled and adored, magnified and revered be thy holy name, Blessed be He with the greatest blessing, hymns, thanksgiving, praise and consolation ever pronounced on earth.» ℞ «Amen.»
>
> «May all Israel's prayers and supplications be gracefully received by thy Father which art in heaven.» ℞ «Amen.»
>
> «May perfect peace descend from heaven and life upon us and all Israel.» ℞ «Amen.»
>
> «May the peace giver in heaven bring peace to us and to all Israel.» ℞ «Amen.»

* * *

The Mishna establishes who can carry out each part of the synagogue service: «Whoever reads the last part of the Prophets can also read the *Šema'* blessing; he shall pass before the Ark and raise his hands. If it is a child, his father or tutor shall pass in his place (for the prayer)» (M Meg 4,5). A child may read the Torah and make its interpretation (*targum*), but he cannot give the *Šema'* blessing, neither may he pass before the Ark, nor raise his hands. A man in rags may give the *Šema'* blessing and its interpretation (targum); but not read the Torah, neither pass before the Ark nor raise his hands. A blind man may give the *Šema'* blessing and act as interpreter. According to R. Judah, he who has never seen the light cannot pronounce the *Šema'* blessing (M Meg 4,6).

CHAPTER VI

SYNAGOGUE PERSONNEL

There was no specially designated personnel to direct synagogue cult, that is, Bible readings, preaching and general prayer. In the first century of our times, these tasks fell to members of the community and this explains how Jesus and Paul, both laymen, could speak in various synagogues. But, although there were no readers, preachers or ministers specially designated to carry out these tasks, it was necessary to count on certain people to supervise things related to divine worship, and to take on different jobs such as maintenance of the building, preparation of cult and internal order at assemblies.

1. THE «ARCHISYNAGOGOS»

Every synagogue had its president or ruler (Heb. *roš ha-kĕneset;* Gr. *arkhisynagôgos*), who is frequently referred to in the New Testament, in Hellenistic Jewish writings and in inscriptions on synagogues and Jewish graves in Palestine and Asia Minor, Greece, Italy, Africa and the Roman Empire in general. This post often coincided in the Diaspore with another, strictly civil, that of archon (Gr. *arkhôn*) or head of the congregation and responsible in general for its direction. Although these were two different posts, they are referred to in a single person in the Gospel according to St. Luke: *arkhôn* (8:41); *arkhisynagôgos* (8:49). The synagogue ruler was usually one of the city's archons. The Talmud, listing this rank in Jewish society, only mentions the synagogue ruler but not the archons. Although both posts could coincide in the same person, the functions or responsibilities were different. In the latter Roman period the ruler of the synagogue was considered leader and official representative of the Jewish community (Epiphany, *Haer.* 30:11; 18; *Codex Theodosianus* XVI, 8,13,14). An inscription in Rome, in Latin and Greek, refers to a person who was archon and synagogue ruler at the same time, although in the Acts of the Apostles (14:2, codex D) these titles do not coincide.

Cfr. CIL X, 3905 = CIJ n. 883: «Alfius Juda arcon, arcosynagogus»; Leon, *Jews of Ancient Rome* n.265: «Stafylo archonti et archysinagogo.»

Little is known of the reasons for electing a synagogue ruler and the way it was done, and we do not know if it was a lifetime job. An inscription found at Acmonia (Frigia) mentions the head of the synagogue with the expression «ruler of the synagogue for life» (Gr. *ho dia biou arkhisinagôgos*). It seems rather that he was named for a certain period of time, probably a year, although he could be reelected if he had inherited the post, if there were only one synagogue ruler — normal practice — or if there were several acting collectively.

Although texts often refer to the synagogue ruler in singular, it is quite usual to find them mentioned in plural, synagogue rulers, in Palestine and in the Diaspore (Mk 5:22; Acts 13:15). The expression *one of the rulers of the synagogue* (Mk 5:22) could be explained as «*one of the ruling class*». In later times the title of synagogue ruler even seems to have been applied to children and women. We must point out that synagogue rulers also appear in pagan rites, but we do not know if this expression was of Jewish or Gentile origin. In the inscription in Apamea precisely three rulers are named.

The ruler of the synagogue was president of the congregation in the strict sense of the word, responsible for keeping order during meetings and for resolving problems; he chose the readers for the Torah and the Prophets and also the preacher (Acts 13:15; M Sot 7,7-8); according to some authors he selected the readings from the prophets for the Sabbath and set the subject for the sermon. At one time the Torah reading seems to have monopolised the service but this abuse of authority was corrected; the *Tosefta'* (Meg

4,21) forbids the reading of the Torah by the synagogue ruler unless the congregation requests it. He played an important part at funerals, judging from the custom in the second century of toasting the health of the synagogue ruler (PT Ber 6a). According to the Ophel inscription, quoted earlier (p. 39-40), the synagogue ruler seems to have been in charge of the administration of the synagogue building together with the head of the community council (Gr. *gerousiarkês*).

The synagogue ruler did not necessarily have to be a scholar; it sufficed that he be educated, familiar with the rites, and capable of judging the capacity of those invited to read the Scriptures, the translation or the sermon. He received no remuneration for this post.

2. THE *HAZZAN*

The word *hazzan,* considered by some to derive from the verb *hazzah* (to see), giving *hazzan* (vigilant), gave rise to comparing the functions of the Jewish *hazzan* with those of the *episkopos* or Christian bishop. This seems excessive in the light of careful study of rabbinical sources that mention him. His functions seem rather to have been similar to those of the first Christian deacons. In the nineteenth century another etymology appeared, derived from Arab *khasin* (keeper of the deposit or store in the synagogue); recently others have seen a derivation from Syrian *hazzanu* (governor or supervisor).

The synagogue ruler had an assistant (Heb. *hazzan ha-kěneset*); undoubtedly the minister (Gr. *hyperetês*) referred to in Lk 4:20, who helped in the daily tasks in the synagogue and in the city. The Talmud mentions two *hăzzanim* necessary for every city (BT Sanh 17b). The *hazzan* acted as chief of ceremonies during the liturgy, bringing the Torah scrolls, calling those selected for reading and for the sermon; he handed the scrolls to the reader and collected them once the reading ended (Lk 4:20; BT Sot 3,7-8; Yom 7,1); he sometimes indicated the moment to reply «Amen» at the end of prayers when the officiant's voice did not reach all the congregation, as happened in large synagogues like the one at Alexandria in Trajan's times. The *hazzan* recited the priest's blessing, word by word, while the priest repeated it after him; at services on public fasting days he gave the sign for sounding the horn and the trumpet after blessings (Sif Nm 39, p. 43; Tos Meg 74b; Tos Ta'an 1,13); he read the prayers and the Scriptures when there was nobody else to do it (PT Ber 12d; Meg 74b; BT Meg 25b); when a collection was made for synagogue funds he declared the amount collected (Lv Rabba 16, p. 357; Ec Rabba 5). He taught the children at school (*bet ha-midraš*) — usually at the synagogue or nearby — when the schoolmaster was absent (M Šab 1,3). He sounded the trumpet Fridays and Sabbath evenings to announce the beginning and end of the day of rest (Tos Sukk 4,199; PT Šab 16a); at small villages he could even act as judge (M Makk 3,12), preacher or schoolmaster (PT Yeb 13a). He accompanied the synagogue ruler as assistant at funerals (PT Ber 6a). The *hazzan,* as we can see, was in all senses at the community's service; he even carried out the sentence on those condemned to whipping (M Makk 3,12).

The *hazzan* was an employee paid by the community and the synagogue. Some synagogues had accommodation for their *hazzan.* Although the *hazzan* did not form part of the group of scholars, he was of higher education than the rest of the population, following the schoolmaster on the city's social scale (M Sot 9,15).

3.   THE MESSENGER

Closely related to the post of *hazzan* was the congregation messenger (Heb. *šeliah sibbur;* Aram. *šěluha' de-sibbura'*). His main task was to recite the prayers out loud so the congregation could follow them.

> The expression *šeliah sibbur* reminds us of the expression in Rev 1:20: angels of the Churches (Gr. *aggeloi tôn ekklêsiôn*).

The congregation messenger was usually considered as a synagogue servant (BT Ber 5,5); the truth is, however, that prayers were not said by a permanent minister but by any member of the congregation. At the beginning this task was carried out by a qualified member of the community invited by the synagogue ruler or the

102

hazzan. When there was no qualified person in the community or whoever was invited declined the invitation to recite the prayers out loud, the *hazzan* took over the job of the congregation messenger. As time went by, the reading of the Scriptures and reciting prayers out loud would become the *hazzan*'s two main tasks, so *hazzan* and *šeliaḥ ṣibbur* became almost synonymous.

Whoever recited prayers had to do it well. The Mishna says: «If the person reciting makes a mistake, it is an ill omen for him. If the person who makes the mistake has been named by the community, it is an ill omen for those who named him, because those who name and he who is named are the same.» It is said that R. Hanina b. Dora, praying for the sick, used to say: «This one will live, this one will die», and he was asked: «How do you know?» He replied: «If I feel the prayer flow from my lips I know he has been accepted, if not, I know he has been turned away» (M Ber 5,5). «If the officiant makes a mistake another person must take his place, with no resistance on his part, and he will begin the section where the former made the mistake» (M Ber 5,3).

4. THE HERALD OF THE ŠEMA ˓

As we have mentioned before, the saying of prayers was preceded by the *Šema˓*. Probably the *Šema˓*, which also included the decalogue (M Tam 4,5; Nash Papyrus), was written on a scroll. The reader or herald of the *Šema˓* (Heb. *paraš 'et šema˓*) was entrusted with unrolling and proclaiming it before the congregation (cf. 1 Tim 2:7 and 2 Tim 1:11), as if it were an imperial edict.

Nevertheless the expression *paraš 'et šema˓* lends itself to a double interpretation: from Aramaean *paraš*, divide, means the division of the *Šema˓* verses in order to be recited as an antiphon by the reader and the congregation; according to others, and this is our interpretation, *paraš 'et sema˓* should be taken in relation to the expression *paraš diatagma*, which means unroll an imperial edict for its proclamation, and thus it would mean public proclamation of the *Šema˓* before the assembly.

5. ALMS COLLECTORS

In cities with a mixed population, where the religious and civil communities were separate, those entrusted with the collecting of alms (Heb. *gabba'i ṣĕdaqah*) were civil servants not related to worship. We can, however, mention them together with synagogue personnel as it was here, in the synagogue, that the alms were collected. There was a difference between the basket for weekly alms (*quppah*), with funds to succour the poor once a week, and the tray (*tmhwy*) from which any needy person, especially strangers, could receive a daily portion. The collection was made by at least two people and the distribution by not less than three.

> The *quppah* was normally a basket for fruit, green vegetables, beans, fish or straw; it was also used to transport large sums of money. The size of the containers suggests that, at the beginning, both *quppah* and *tmhwy* were used to collect offerings in kind, as well as money.

6. THE 'EŚREH BATLANIM, AND THE SINGER

We cannot complete the list of synagogue personnel without a mention of the ten men out of work (Heb. *'eśreh batlanim*) who agreed, for a sum of money, especially in post-Talmudical Judaism, to attend the synagogue services so that there would be the *minyan* or the minimum ten members necessary to constitute an assembly. This measure is completely foreign to Mishna times, although the term appears in some of its passages (cf. BT Meg 1,3: What is considered a large town? One where there are ten men out of work. If there are less, it is considered a village). The expression *'eśreh batlanim,* however, must have been used to refer to individuals whose occupations did not prevent them from attending the synagogue, even on weekdays. So it is only a characteristic of large towns to always be able to find, even during the week, the required number for official synagogue worship.

As time went by a figure that did not exist originally was added to the traditional personnel: the professional singer, later known by the name of Byzantian origin *payyĕṭan* (Heb. *payyeṭanim,* in plural). The idea of this singer was to make prayers more attractive and intense on special days and to give greater solemnity to synagogue worship.

The rite or order of synagogue service on the Sabbath and feast days, the functions and the personnel have remained unchanged throughout the times with only slight modifications or additions.

7. DRESS AND ITS COMPLEMENTS

Dress

As far as the Jews' dress is concerned, both the Old and New Testaments, but particularly the New, mention cloak, toga, tunic, belt and footwear, as well as underclothes or a cloth, a kind of breeches, longer or shorter, rolled round the loins.

The Palestinian Talmud (Meg 73d) mentions special clothes to be worn when reading the different parts of the Scriptures.

Dress complements

As accessories or complements to dress, almost pure ornamentation, we will make special reference to the phylacteries and hems.

The phylacteries

The word phylactery comes from Greek *phylaktêrion* and means an object that protects or guards (some written fragments of the Torah); phylacteries are called in Hebrew *tĕfillim,* derived perhaps from *tĕfillah,* prayer. During morning prayer (except on the Sabbath; cf. BT Šab 5b; M Šab 6,2) all adult Jews should wear on their left arm (close to the heart) and on the forehead, two cubical leather cases, each of which contained in writing on narrow parchments four essential passages from the Law (Dt 6:8; cf. Ex 13:9,16; Dt 11:18), among them part of the *Šema'* (Ex 13:1-10,11-13; Dt

6:4-9; 11:13-21). The ones on the arms should contain four Biblical passages and those on the head should have four compartments, containing the four passages in the stipulated order (Mekilta to Ex 13,15, p. 74). Some devoted wore them all day. This custom, still followed by Orthodox Jews, originated from a literal interpretation of Dt 6:8, as we have explained earlier. In the Gospel according to St. Matthew (23:5) Jesus criticizes excess and ostentation which led to enlarged phylacteries. The Mekilta to Exodus 13:9 (p. 68) sets out the rules for wearing phylacteries on one's head and left arm, and adds: «Wearing phylacteries is like reading the Torah and he who reads the Torah is dispensed from wearing phylacteries.» The Mishna establishes that a person who does not wear phylacteries (imposed by the Torah) is not guilty; but he who has five compartments in his phylacteries is guilty as he goes against the rabbi's words (M Ber 3,1).

A priest with deformed arms is dispensed from wearing phylacteries on them; R. Judah also dispensed people whose hands had purple (indigo) or ruby marks, as the congregation's attention would be drawn to them (M Meg 4,7). Women, slaves and children were also dispensed and those in mourning (M Ber 3,1).

Phylacteries should be put on before reciting the *Šema˙* (PT Ber 4c) and should be protected from all impurities. The *Berakot* tractate reflects the Shammaites' and Hillelites' opinion on what should be done with the phylacteries if it were necessary to visit the lavatory: the Shammaites think they should be removed four cubits from the entrance to the lavatory, placed in a niche outside and, on leaving, should be put on arms and head again four cubits away from the lavatory; the Hillelites, on the other hand, believe they should be carried in one's hand on entering the lavatory. R. Aqiba said they should be wrapped in one's clothes before entering (BT Ber 22a).

Fringes or borders

Nm 15:38-41 instructs the Israelites to put fringes (Heb. *ṣiṣit;* Gr. *kraspedon*) round the edges of their dress and, at each end of the fringes, a purple, sky blue or violet cord to remind them of

God's commandments (Nm 15:38ff; cf. Ez 8:3); four cords were normally used for this: three white and one violet. These cords were slipped round the edge of the cloak and tied in a special, complicated way. The ends that were left hanging should be at least three fingers (Hillel) or four fingers (Shammai) long and sometimes, for show, they were left even longer.

In the New Testament fringes and borders are mentioned on the hem of Jesus' dress (Mt 9:20 and par.; 14:36 and par.) or on the Pharisees' (Mt 23:5). The were used to denote their piety (Mt 9:20; Lk 8:44; Mt 14:36; Mk 6:56) and even to attract attention (Mt 23:5).

Every male Israelite was obliged to wear fringes. According to R. Meir «the blue or violet cord is like the sea, which is like the sky, which is like God's throne» (BT Sot 17a). It was because of this religious meaning that the sick touched the hem of Jesus' dress (Mt 9:20; 14:36; Mk 6:56; Lk 8:44).

Rabbinical instructions on fringes appear in the fourth tractate of the seven that were added to the Palestinian Talmud.

CHAPTER VII

OTHER USES OF THE SYNAGOGUE

1. SYNAGOGUE AND SCHOOL

The basic educational institution among the Jews was the Synagogue, which was used as a place for meeting and worship.

From the very beginning Scripture reading and Torah instruction were the central point for Sabbath meetings and these gave an educational character to the synagogue as an institution. For Philo and Flavius Josephus the synagogue is mainly a place for instruction, a «school of philosophy». According to Flavius Josephus, Moses ordered children «to begin by studying the laws, the most beautiful of lessons and fount of joy» (*Ant.* IV, 8,12 [211]). He ordered children to be instructed in the rudiments of knowledge (reading and writing) and to be taught the laws and deeds of their forefathers; the latter to initiate, and the former so that, growing up in them, they would not break them or have the excuse of ignorance (*Apion,* II, 25 [204]). Referring to himself, Josephus was proud of the fact that at 14 years of age he was as versed in the Law as the High Priest, and prominent men of Jerusalem came to him to ask for «precise information on certain points of our laws» (*Vita,* 2 [9]).

In the *Pirke Abot* the following phases are established in a man's life in Jewish society: «He can study the Scriptures at five years of age, the Mishna at ten, the Talmud at fifteen and he can marry from eighteen onwards, at twenty he is ready for work; at thirty he has strength, at forty intelligence, at fifty counsel, at sixty (rabbinic) maturity, at seventy aged (white hair), at eighty advanced age, at ninety he leans and at a hundred it is if he were dead, absent and far from the world» (*Abot*

5,21). It is said of Jesus that at twelve he showed himself to be in possession of outstanding knowledge (Lk 2:41-52). In the Qumran community, marriage was put off till the age of twenty (1QSa). If any formal education existed it would take place from eighteen years of age onwards.

One of the basic beliefs of post-exile Judaism was that knowledge of the Torah was the highest objective in life and its learning deserved the maximum effort. There are numerous texts of *Pirke Abot* that are insistent on this point. R. Hillel said: «An ignorant man cannot be pious» (*Abot* 2,6). He also used to say: «More study of the Torah, more life; more investigation, more knowledge; more advice, more reasonable conduct... All who obtain knowledge of the Torah, obtain life in the future world» (*Abot* 2,7). R. Šammai said: «Make (the study of) the Torah a regular occupation», and R. Hananias: «If two sit down together and do not discuss the Torah, it is a meeting of the scornful for it is written (Ps 1:1): "Blessed is the man that walketh not in the council of the ungodly... nor sitteth in the seat of the scornful". But if two sit together and discuss the Torah, then *Šěkinah* is present among them, for it is written (Mal 3:16): "Then they that feared the Lord spake often one to another: and the Lord hearkened, and heard it". And he who studies the Scriptures is considered to have complied with all the Torah» (*Abot* 3,3; cf. 3,6).

We have already mentioned the 480 synagogues that existed in Jerusalem according to rabbinical tradition, each of them with a *bet ha-šefer* (book house or school) for reading the Torah (*miqra'* = Scripture) and a *bet ha-midraš* for its subsequent study (M Meg 3,1; PT Meg 73d).

> The Hebrew expression *bet ha-midraš* (Gr. *oikos paideias)* for school appears as soon as Eclo 51:23,29.

Although learning to read was quite common, this was not so much the case with the rather more difficult art of writing. In the ruins of Qumran an ostracon appeared with a complete alphabet which seems to be «an exercise for a scribe student».

The study house (*bet ha-midraš*), generally conceived for teaching the young, was considered in the third century more of an institution parallel to the synagogue than an integral part of it. We do not know if this was so in the first century as Jesus and Paul appear teaching in the synagogue but the New Testament makes no mention at all of the *bet ha-midraš*. («The school of Tyrannus» in Acts 19:9 can hardly be identified with the *bet ha-midraš* at Ephesus.)

It seems that children did not learn to read directly from the Law scrolls but with small boards or scrolls that contained certain sections of the Scripture (*Šema'*, etc.; cf. Naš Papyrus). This basic instruction was received in the school-master's house. It was only when children reached the age of being taught Scripture reading in the synagogue were they taken to the *bet ha-šefer*. There, the teacher, who had no Torah scrolls available at home, took the child to the room where they were kept in the synagogue and prepared the Sabbath reading with him under the supervision of the *hazzan*, who acted as teacher when nobody else was available to do so (M Šab 1,3).

Thus the term *bet ha-midraš* does not refer to a school of higher grade but rather to a place for all who wanted to become expert in the explanation of the Law. Here, besides the scrolls of the Torah and the Prophets scrolls, which were read at the Sabbath ceremony, there were also some Midraš or Halaka scrolls and some of the Pešer, available only to a restricted circle.

2. THE SYNAGOGUE, A PLACE FOR COMMUNITY MEETINGS

The use of the synagogue, not just as a place for prayer and learning, but also as a centre for community meetings, goes back to Talmudical times. This function was reinforced as time went by under the *ghetto* conditions in which Jewish communities found themselves involved.

There was no daily activity of the Jews that was not to be found reflected in synagogue life. Anyone who had a personal accusation or claim against another should stop attending synagogue services until reconciliation had taken place; verdicts and sentences from law suits, objects lost, stolen or found, sale and purchase of certain

111

objects on the market — everything was announced in the synagogue.

In Italy in the Middle Ages, when someone decided to leave the community he had to announce it publicly so that anyone could present claims; in the synagogue the banns were read to reinforce moral and conjugal virtues; mourners were publicly and officially consoled; the presence of a couple on the Sabbath, before or after the wedding, was an occasion for joy on the part of the community.

The punishment with greatest social pressure was *herem* or excommunication which, among other things, excluded the person from the congregation (Ezr 10:8). Apparently the penalty of excommunication was not imposed by the people but by the elders of the congregation or by Jewish authorities (cf. Jn 9:22).

From Qumran documents (1QS 6-7) we learn the different penalties established for those who committed infractions. Expulsion from the community could be temporary or permanent: three months for talking nonsense (7,9), up to sixty days for being unable to make good some harm caused accidentally (7,10) or a minimum of ten days for interrupting a speaker (7,9-10) or making signs with one's left hand (7,15). Temporary expulsion by way of exclusion from the common table could last one to two years. A year's exclusion was imposed for lying in matters concerning property (6,24-25), for disobeying one's superiors (6,25-27), for raising one's voice to a priest (7,2-3), or for speaking ill of him (7,15-16). Two years exclusion — the first from «purity» and the second from «drink» — were imposed on a former member before he could be readmitted (7,18-20). For more serious transgressions, like pronouncing God's name (6,27-7,2), slandering the congregation (7,16-17), abandoning the community after having been a member for more than ten years (7,22-24) and sharing food or possessions with a person who had been excommunicated (7,24-25) the sentence was permanent excommunication.

In a separate catalogue referring to members of the community council or sacred council, permanent excommunication is the penalty established for breaking any of Moses' laws (1QS 8,21-23); transgressions from heedlessness are punished in this case by two years' exclusion from community activity (8,24-9,2). There can be no doubt that two types of excommunication existed as part of the legal system to which the Dead Sea manuscripts bear witness.

112

3. THE SYNAGOGUE, A CENTRE FOR SOCIAL ATTENTION

Another ancient function of the synagogue was as a centre for social attention, as a place to receive strangers, with lodgings for them. The Talmud justifies the reciting of the Kidduš in the synagogue, in spite of the fact that the Kidduš should only be recited at meals, maintaining this practice because visitors and travellers ate, drank and slept in the synagogue (Peš 101a). This mention does not of course refer to the prayer hall, as it was expressly forbidden to eat and drink here (BT Meg 28a); it refers rather to a room adjoining the synagogue that served as a dining hall; in chapter II we have quoted the Veteno inscriptions, from the first century of our era, where it says that he also constructed: «the guest-house and rooms and installations for water to attend the needs of those who come from far away». In Jerusalem ruins of the Alexandrian synagogue have been discovered, and these were also used to lodge pilgrims that came to the baths.

> The use of the synagogue as a centre for social assistance grew during the Middle Ages and is specially important in today's synagogues, above all in the United States.

We can summarize by saying that the synagogue building was made the most of, not only for Sabbath or mid-week services; it soon became the place for education for children and youngsters, for community meeting and centre for social attention. Because of its multiple functions, the synagogue and its adjoining installations could vary greatly in size, according to the necessities of each community.

PART II

THE CORDOBA SYNAGOGUE

CHAPTER VIII

MEDIAEVAL SPANISH SYNAGOGUES

1.   SYNAGOGUE BUILDINGS IN THE MIDDLE AGES

The Jews scattered throughout the world adopted the architectural style of each country when the moment came to construct buildings, making the necessary adaptations to meet their own needs.

In the Middle Ages the Jewish communities were small groups of people, and this explains the reduced size of their synagogues, which were sometimes simply a room for public prayer. The ancient synagogues in Palestine were usually small too (p. 55).

The circumstances of insecurity and external pressure under which many Jewish communities lived in the Middle Ages also influenced and conditioned the model and construction of their buildings. It was not to be wondered that the Catholic Church forbade the building of a new synagogue in certain places and even the enlargement of existing ones... The rule reflected in the Talmud that «the synagogue should be higher than the surrounding buildings» (BT Šab 11a) could not be put into practice as ecclesiastical laws ruled that such buildings be lower than churches. To give the prayer hall extra height it became the custom to set the synagogue floor beneath street level so the synagogues would not appear to be high buildings, but at the same time Psalm 130:1 would be put into practice literally: «Out of the depths have I cried unto thee, O Lord.» Until the eighteenth century the outside appearance of the synagogues was modest, with rare exceptions, their beauty being concentrated inside.

In the Middle Ages the layout of the space inside the synagogues

117

centred traditionally round three points: the *'aron* or ark of the Torah, the *bimah,* a kind of platform or pulpit, and the space reserved for worshipers. Following the custom in Palestinian apsidal synagogues (p. 44), in many synagogues in the diaspore the ark was placed in a niche in the eastern wall facing Jerusalem, called *hekal* (= temple or shrine).

The *bimah* occupied a prominent position inside the synagogue and it was from here that the synagogue services were conducted. The proximity of the place for the ark on the east wall and the place for the *bimah,* endeavouring to strike a balance between them, is still one of the problems presented today in the distribution of the synagogue's inner space.

In order to separate men and women during prayer, mediaeval synagogues adopted two solutions that had been used in ancient Palestinian synagogues: in some cases the custom of building a gallery on the upper floor was adopted (p. 71) as in the Córdoba and Tránsito (in Toledo) synagogues, both fourteenth century; in others, a space or room adjoining the prayer hall on the same level or sometimes below its level was the solution adopted, it seems, in some ancient synagogues that had no women's gallery (p. 72). Usually, in the Mediaeval period, the space reserved for women was a room built onto the synagogue building.

From an artistic point of view, Spanish mediaeval synagogues formed part of Islamic civilization. For their decoration the Jews used verses from the Bible, written in elegant Spanish Hebrew characters, imitating in this way the decoration of mosques with verses from the Koran.

2. THE TOLEDO SYNAGOGUES

No synagogue from the golden age of Spanish Judaism (X-XII centuries) stands today; the ones still preserved — two in Toledo (Santa María la Blanca and the Tránsito) and one in Córdoba — are later (XIII and XIV centuries).

Santa María la Blanca

History

The Santa María la Blanca synagogue appears to have been built in 1203 by Ibn Šušan; although some, like the architect Czekelius, maintain it was built between 1250 and 1300 (CB 45), basing this claim on the Granada style architectural influence. In any case, the decoration in this synagogue appears to be later than 1203. According to L. Torres Balbas (quoted by CB 64), this decoration indicates «advanced period within XIII century, who compares it with certain Mudéjar plasters at the Huelgas in Burgos, dated in 1275».

The synagogue was used for Jewish worship until the second decade of this century when it was converted into a church with the name of Santa María la Blanca.

As far as its conversion into a Christian church is concerned, Francisco de Pisa in his *Descripción de ... Toledo* (quoted by CB 59) says: «It seems that St. Vicente Ferrer "arriving at this city of Toledo, seeing the obstination, disbelief and treachery of some, taking with him some armed people, entered the Jewish quarter ... and in the ancient temple now called Santa María la Blanca (which was their synagogue) and in spite of all the Jews, he blessed it, and, turning them out, he made it a church ... and celebrated Mass in it. To commemorate this event every year a solemn procession comes from the Santiago del Arrabal church to Santa María la Blanca, because the inhabitants of that parish were the ones who accompanied the saint, armed for that occasion: as would be recorded in more detail in the description of the Churches in Toledo"...» Cantera comments (p. 59) that the legends attributing a violent intervention to St. Vicente Ferrer have no historical basis whatsoever.

During the second half of the XVI century the synagogue was the church for the monastery founded by Cardinal Silíceo to take in reformed penitent women, and the three chapels in the present sanctuary belong to that period. From 1600 to 1791 it became a hermitage or congregation, being transformed into barracks in 1791. In 1798 Don Vicente Domínguez de Prado, intendent to the royal army and general of the Toledo province, restored it and made it a deposit for articles belonging to the royal estate. In 1851 it underwent another restoration, and was later declared a national monument.

Santa María la Blanca is, in J. Amador de los Ríos' opinion (*Historia* I, 451) «the most beautiful and magnificent synagogue ever owned by the Jews in the Península», and according to Lambert (quoted by CB 58) «a monument of exceptional value in the history of Spanish-Arabic art and of quite unique interest in Spain».

Description

The architectural layout of the Santa María la Blanca synagogue corresponds to the basilica type, with five naves covered with a plain panelled ceiling of decreasing height (from 12.50 metres in the central nave to 10 in the next, and 7 in the furthest ones). The naves are separated by four rows of octagonal columns with beautiful capitels, different from each other, with oriental cones as a special feature above which rear beautiful and elegant wrought iron arches. Windows opened on the eastern wall appear to have communicated with the women's galleries, no longer preserved. Thus the body of the synagogue, according to Czekelius (quoted by CB 62), was longer, as the wall which today is the facade is merely the opening onto the women's gallery filled in. In spite of its reduced size (26 to 28 ms. long by 19 to 23 ms. wide), the inside šeems spacious, the combination of columns and arches giving the illusion of amplitude. An Andalusian decorator, according to Gómez Moreno (quoted by CB 63) «enriched the work with plasters, converting pillars into columns with splendid capitels, adorned with "albanegas" (triangles formed by arches), where round oval bas-relief abound with ornamented plaster-work, and over them stretched friezes with loops and blind arches, to the top of the walls, where Hebrew inscriptions never came to be carved on murals that today are empty, and could simply have been painted; but all polychromatic decoration disappeared with a general whitewashing, which justifies the name given to its Christian title» (Saint Mary the White).

120

The Tránsito (or Prince's) synagogue

History

The other Toledo synagogue, the Tránsito synagogue, was built around 1357 (?) in times of Don Pedro el Cruel, as a private prayer chamber for his Treasury minister Samuel ha-Levi Abulafia. On his death (1360) it was put at the Church's disposal. As from 1494 it was in the hands of the Calatrava Order, who turned it into a chapel at first for the San Benito priorship and later for the State. On its floor the tombstones of some of its knights can still be seen today. With the decline of military orders it was reduced to a hermitage dedicated to the Tránsito de Nuestra Señora from the XVIII century (containing the Calatrava and Alcántara Orders' archives). During the Napoleonic Wars it was used as military barracks and on 1st May 1877 it was declared a national monument (eight years before the Córdoba synagogue).

Description

The luxury of this synagogue's interior decoration, fit for the great hall of a palace according to Lambert (quoted by CB 77), contrasts with the sober outside appearance: mere walls of brick and mortar, with no more decoration apart from bracket cornices and Mudéjar windows with arches. The inside is sumptuous and its structure of fine brick is covered with stucco.

The synagogue's sole entrance is at the extreme south-east of the southern wall, with an entrance hall of seven by four metres. The inside is rectangular, 23 ms. long by 9.05 wide. The walls are profusely decorated with Moorish engravings, especially on the eastern wall where the altar for the Christian chapel was later installed: filigrees, sinuous floral stems, vine shoots and leaves and «flor de lis» alternating with lines of verses from the Psalms. On the southern wall there are large rectangular spaces which correspond to the women's galleries. Above the women's galleries the present windows would be opened and along the front wall is a wide frieze of heraldic castles set among floral motifs terminating in borders, loops and Arabic inscriptions of ancient style.

121

The *western wall* presents similar decoration. Along the top it has eight lobular arches, the two at each end having been closed off and the four central ones open with lattices; at a certain distance on each side a large window with an ogive arch completes the wall.

But the most sumptuous and exuberant examples of decoration were deposited by Toledo craftsmen on the eastern wall, round the niche for the ark or *hekal* (Hebrew word which means temple, used by Sephardies to refer to the place destined for the ark in which the Torah scrolls were kept): three vertical panels with rectangular frame, the central one having its lower part perforated by three arches over columns with curious capitels. These three arches would form the niche for the Torah ark. There are inscriptions on either side in remembrance of Samuel ha-Levi Abulafia, who constructed the building. This place is illuminated by natural light filtering through windows opened on the opposite, western wall. The cornice is underlined by a long Hebrew inscription containing verses from the Psalms and praising King Don Pedro I, as it was he who gave permission for its construction. In the synagogue there are several coats of arms from Castille and Leon as well as various Hebrew inscriptions with fragments from the Psaltery.

* * *

Later than Santa María la Blanca (1203) and earlier than Tránsito (a. 1357), the Córdoba synagogue was built and patronized towards 1315 by Yishaq Moheb, according to an inscription on its eastern wall. The final chapters of this book are dedicated to this synagogue which is of smaller dimensions than the Toledo ones.

CHAPTER IX

THE JEWS IN CORDOBA

We do not know the exact date from which groups of Jews have lived in Spain. Different legends, almost all of them mediaeval, assure us that the Jews had settled in the Peninsula since Solomon's times (X century B.C.). However, the first absolutely reliable epigraphical evidence of a family of Palestininan origin, inhabitant of Hispania, dates from the second century of our era. This first sign is an *epitaph to Justinus,* originally from the Palestinian city of Nablus (Samaria). As from the fourth century of our era we have copious documentary evidence of the existence of a flourishing community of Jews in Spain.

1. X-XII CENTURIES

In the X-XII centuries Spanish Judaism saw a vigorous revival in Córdoba, the capital of al-Andalus or Moslem Spain. With the coming to power of Abd-ar-Rahman III, as Caliph (929) a policy of reconciliation was initiated which favoured the Córdoba Jewish community, recognizing a people who were particularly loyal and giving rise to a period of cultural development which was most beneficial. In al-Andalus Jewish communities sprang up all over the place with cities like Lucena and Granada where the population was mostly Jewish. To a large degree this revival was undoubtedly due to Hasday ben Šaprut, Jewish minister to Abd-ar-Rahman III and nasi or head of the Jewish communities in al-Andalus.

With the caliph's fall (1031) the party kingdoms (*reinos de taifas*) began, which from a cultural point of view favoured the sciences and arts, initiating the golden age of Andalusian Judaism towards mid XI century. On the death of Almanzor's son, al-Muzaffar, anarchy and insecurity take over.

2. XIII-XV CENTURIES

Jewish influence in the city declined at the end of the caliph period, but revived once again when the city was conquered by Ferdinand III (29th June 1236) and the law which judicially consolidated the conquest was proclaimed. This jurisdiction was soon replaced by privileges, royal edicts and municipal statutes (EC 85-86). After the conquest the Jews found themselves protected by a policy of Christian tolerance which enabled them to recover part of the splendour lost under Almoravide and Almohade rule.

Following Ferdinand III, Alphonse III, the Wise, endeavoured to improve the lot of the Jews, granting them privileges and rights of different kinds: «They may have all offices and honours that all Christians have» reads the text of law VI from the XXIV title of the seventh section of the book of the *Siete Partidas* by the Wise King; in Granada, Córdoba and Seville their quarters and dwellings were enlarged and surrounded with walls, and the reconstruction of synagogues was authorized with certain restrictions on the decoration to be used in them (Law IV/from XXIV title, seventh section of the book of the *Siete Partidas;* cf. Amador de los Ríos, *Estudios sobre los Judíos de España,* p. 36).

The Jews' behaviour attracted the attention of Popes Gregory IX and Innocence IV who, in 1240 and 1250 respectively, issued bulls ordering them to wear a mark on their clothes to identify them (RB 238, n.2). Innocence IV ordered the destruction of a sumptuous synagogue being built in Córdoba, as we have seen, as it broke the law in vigour «with dishonour and great scandal to Christianity».

Some Córdoba authors assume the Córdoba synagogue that can be visited today to be the one whose destruction was ordered by Innocence IV. Thus Gómez Bravo states that «Innocence IV ordered its destruction in a bull issued in Leon in France on 13th April 1250, to Don Gutierre Ruiz Dolea, at that time Bishop of Córdoba; but he does not know — he adds — if this order reached Don Gutierre in time, as on 15th June that same year the bishopric of Córdoba was vacant» (*Catálogo de Obispos,* volume I, p. 269). Sánchez de Feria states that it was demolished, being reduced to the «humble construction seen today» referring to the Greek-Roman restoration which hid the Mudéjar plasters that decorate the synagogue's walls today (*Palestra sagrada,* volume IV, p. 411). However, Romero Barros (pp. 240-241) does not share this opinion.

The decree by Innocence IV has precedents in two canons by St. Gregory the Great and Alexander III recorded in chapter VI of *Corpus de las decretales* by Gregorio IX, sent to the Universities of Bologne (1230) and París (1234) and compiled by St. Raimundo de Peñafort. These canons refer to the Jews and are an excellent illustration of the Church's attitude during the Roman-Visigoth period and the reconquest in the Middle Ages: Jews are not allowed to build new synagogues, but they may preserve the old ones, on the condition that the restoration does not mean enlarging them or improving their former appearance.

Canon by St. Gregory the Great (y. 600): «3. Sicut legalis definitio (cf. *Codex of Justinianus,* book I, title X, law 19) Judaeos novas non patitur erigere synagogas, ita eos sine inquietudine veteres habere permittit.»
Canon by Alexander III (y. 1180): «7. Judaeos de novo construere synagogas ubi non habuerunt pati non debes. Verum, si antiquae corruerint vel ruinam minantur, ut eas reaedificent potest aequanimiter tolerari; non autem ut eas exaltent, aut campliores, aut pretiosores faciant quam antea fuisse noscuntur: qui utique pro magno debent habere quod in veteribus synagogis et suis observantiis tolerantur» (FF 362).

Meanwhile, canonical law on synagogues had remained standing and in force, as shown by the civil law in Partida VII, 24,4: «Synagogue is the house where the Jews make prayer. And this house, as it is, cannot be remade in any place within our dominion except by our order; but those that are of old, if it should happen that they fall down, can be repaired and made on that same land in the same fashion as they were before, not making them longer nor higher... And the synagogue made in another fashion, the Jews should forfeit it and it belong to the high church of the place where it be made» (FF 378).

The Partida laws gave no more protection to the restoration of synagogues than that prescribed by canonical law, but this Partidas code, drawn up between 1256 and 1263, did not come legally into force until 1348, when it began to be applied with full vigour. An example, quoted by Fita (p. 380) «it is a true record (3rd April 1379), whereby the queen, Doña Juana, wife of Enrique II, acting as Lady of the Manor at Valencia de Don Juan» (León province, Oviedo diócesis) orders her mayors to abide by the "laws, which apply in this case, where it says that the Jews cannot make new synagogues, nor ennoble the old ones more than they were before; and if this were done the Jews should forfeit them, and they should belong to the Church"». The synagogue in that «aljama» which indeed was confiscated for use as the parochial church, had been «a house of prayer, small; and later they made it much larger and nobler and more splendid than it was at first, and of much greater value than the parish where it was located». The law, for all that, was not so harsh as it may seem, for when the embargo or surrender of the building took place «the said mayors commanded the said Jews to take out of the synagogue the lamps and the Torahs, and the other things that they had in the said synagogue; for they said they did not make any embargo on them» (FF 380).

Limits of the Córdoba Jewish quarter or «aljama»

In the Middle Ages the Jews congregated in communities called *kahal* in Hebrew and «aljama» in Spanish, a word that came from Arab *ỹamā'a*, «group of people» (esp. *ỹamā'at al-yahūd*, «group of Jews»). These communities, concentrated in a quarter, had their own community organisation, for very often the members of the *kahal* or «aljama» were authorized by governors to regulate the political, civil and religious life of the community members, although they were subject to various kinds of restrictions according to the different places and governors.

Córdoba was conquered by Ferdinand III on 29th June 1236 and the keys of the city were handed over to him by prince Abu-l-

Hasan who surrendered under a capitulation agreed after a more or less prolonged resistance.

Indeed the text of the first Crónica General de España reads: «And Córdoba was closely besieged... and then, suffering the inhabitants of the city from attacks and battles made against them, and faint from hunger and lack of vittals... they were forced to deliver themselves up to king Don Ferdinand. And the Arabians... came out with their bodies whole, no more, to flee» (González Jiménez, M., *En torno a los orígenes de Andalucía: La Repoblación del siglo XIII*, Publicaciones de la Universidad de Sevilla 1980, 39-40, quoted by LO 103).

After the conquest, «the Moslems left freely, taking their movable furniture and belongings with them, forfeiting their unmovable goods (houses and land) which would be the object of donations and sharing out among conquerors and populators, and leaving the conquered place immediately». Córdoba falling under Castillian power «more than a symbol, it was the reality of Islam's elimination as a strong political power in the Península» (cf. EC 78, who describes in detail the conquest of the city by Ferdinand III in two stages [1236-1240 and 1240-1241] as well as its jurisdicial consolidation by statute, pp. 62-87).

On 30th June, Ferdinand III, surrounded by the nobility and the whole population, made his solemn entry into the city. After celebrating Mass, the monarch went straight to the Alcázar built by the Moslems, commencing at once to make the necessary arrangements with the nobility to populate the city with Christians, being now empty of Moslems. As from this moment the greater part of the population would be made up of Christians, both nobility and common people.

Nevertheless, Christian documents from the period frequently mention the Mudejars — from Arab *mudeȳȳen*, literally «he who has been allowed to remain» past participle of the second form of *daȳan*, remain — although we do not know in which quarter or quarters they lived nor the number of inhabitants (Orti Belmonte, M. A., *Fuero*, 47ff). They formed an ethnic religious minority in the city, although they were fewer in number than the Jews and their community was not subjected to such violent attacks as the latter's.

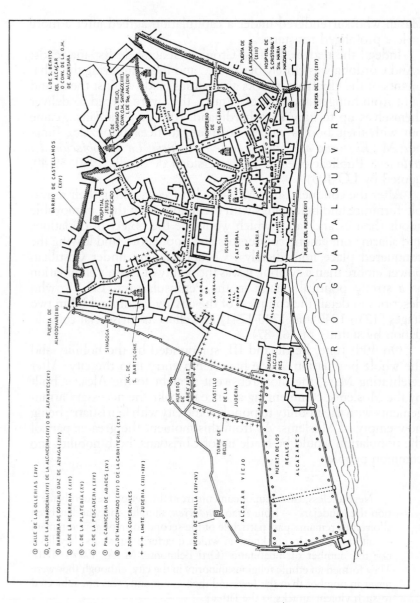

Map of the Santa María quarter during the lower Middle Ages; cf. J. M. Escobar
Camacho's Doctoral Thesis, La ciudad de Córdoba en la baja Edad Media
Córdoba, 1987, Map No. 7

After the conquest the Jewish population continued in the city in this period in the traditional «aljama» from Arab times — the Judería — situated also in the Madina, as is shown by the donation of some houses by Ferdinand III to the bishopric in 1241, and whose limits are referred to «ad viam que descendit de maburget contra vicum iudeorum» (LO 105). This quarter covered the urban space existing between the Almodóvar gate, the Cathedral and the Bishop's houses, including «the Judería Castle, Almohade alcázar of old, which today forms part of the Alcázar Viejo» district set in the SW. angle of the town, as an extension of the Córdoba precinct first mentioned in 1359. When Juan II mentions this fortification in 1449 he says: «the said castle used to be Jewish.» The castle is contiguous to the Alcázar Viejo, but different, limiting what would later be the San Basilio quarter and is so called at least until 1515. On the other hand, the Judería is attacked in 1391, the motive being robbery and pillage, and not to kill Jews as has been supposed earlier (Nieto Cumplido, M. and Luca de Tena y Alvear, C., «El Alcázar Viejo, una repoblación cordobesa del siglo XIV», *Axerquía* 1 [1980] 240-241). But as Christians and Jews lived side by side in the Judería and the assault was followed by conversions, this area was not depopulated because of these events, although some people moved to other parts of the city, for example, to the parish of San Nicolás de la Axerquía. In 1478 the corregidor, Don Francisco Valdés, obliged the Jews to live in the Alcázar Viejo quarter, but they protested to the King, who by royal letter in 1479, gave them permission to live in their old precinct, where they remained until the expulsion. The Royal Decree by Ferdinand the Catholic dated 16th May 1479 is expressed in the following terms:

«Be it known that on the part of *the Aljama and Jews of this said city* their request was referred to me, which was presented before me in my council, saying that having, as they have, *all the Jews who live and dwell in the said city of Córdoba, their dwellings close by their synagogue, and being apart,* having on one side and on the other *two ancient arches* where, if gates were fixed to them, the Jews would be enclosed; and having Doctor de Prado and Doctor Talavera from my Council, and Ferrán Alvarez, my Secretary, on my command gone to see where the said Jews dwelt, whether they were apart from conversation and dealings with Christians and contained within their judería, being myself and my very dear wife, in this same city, it was agreed that the said Jews should remain in the judería where they were and that *two gates in the said arches* should be installed so that they be more apart and enclosed; and having the Corregidor mediated the said gates in seven thousand maravedis, and being the aforesaid in this state, you, the said Francisco de Valdés, my Corregidor, moved and induced by certain persons, have ordered under threat of punishment that the said Jews leave *their houses and Judería and Synagogue* and go to live in the *Alcázar Viejo where you, the said Corregidor, dwell;* in which you say they are very aggravated, because their being, as they are, apart, they should not be ordered to leave their houses and judería and synagogue, and to go and buy other houses and make another new synagogue in another place because they would leave all their belongings and would have nothing with which to maintain themselves nor buy houses and new synagogue; on their behalf I was asked and begged for mercy's sake to dispose as my mercy saw fit.»

«Having been considered in my Council and discussed with me, for information was given that the said doctors and Ferrán Alvarez viewed the place and concluded that it was a suitable place for the Jews to remain there and be apart, it was considered that I give you this letter of mine in this sense; and I agreed. Thus I now command you, that you may later be notified in it, to have installed *in the said arches, that are at the entrance to the Judería, its gates to close and to open;* and if you should consider it necessary to put more gates, to have them put also; and let the said Jews be in the said judería as they are now, and not constrain them or compel them to go, and to live in any other part, nor to have to withdraw from the said Alcázar Viejo; and if some are or were outside the said place, urge and compel them to enter once more into the said precinct, so no Christian dwell nor live in the said precinct; and no Jew live any longer outside it, notwithstanding any rule, with the punishment you may have put on it; which I lift and remove from them with the present ruling, and I free and discharge them; neither shall you do them harm *nor allow it to be done to them, nor any injury nor any other offence to their persons, nor to their goods, as should not be done; for with this my letter I take the Jews under my care and protection and royal defence;* and neither the ones nor the others should do any of these things, under penalty of my mercy and of ten thousand maravedis for my Council, etc. Given in the town of Cáceres, on the sixteenth day of March, year of Jesus Christ our Saviour fourteen seventy nine» (quoted by FF 394-395).

The Judería coincided more or less with the following streets: Judíos, where the synagogue is, Albucasis, Manríquez, Averroes, Judería, Almanzor, Tomás Conde, Deanes, Romero; and the squares: Cardenal Salazar, Judá Leví and Maimónides, a quarter that in 1292 Alphonse X ordered to be closed in, obliging its inhabitants to live within its limits (LO 105). So the quarter extended as far as the Almodóvar gate, on the left of which, according to Ramírez de Arellano (*Paseos,* 576, n. 958), on the land occupied by the King's garden, the Jews had their Cemetery, and so this place was called *Fonsario de los Judíos* (Jews' Graveyard). The Judería was separated from the rest of the city by a walled precinct, of which we do not know the complete site. This precinct was entered by two gates: the Judería gate, situated opposite the north-west angle of the Cathedral-Mosque, and the Malburguete gate whose even approximate position we ignore (EC 191ff). But not all the Jews lived in this quarter. Confined to this Jewish quarter at the beginning, very soon after 1260 some of them also settled in Christian houses situated in areas close by it, and later in commercial sites in the city, in the quarter of San Salvador and San Andrés, which shows they could move freely about the city. By the decree, the Jews in Córdoba were subject to Christians judicially and politically, and could not hold any post, except that of «almojarife» (tax collector) to the King. The fact that a Jew could collect the king's rents and tarifs is proof of the absolute confidence he had in their economic dealings. Urban segregation of the Judería was maintained until 1391, when the assault and pillage occurred, causing the disappearance of the Judería as an urban sector separated from the rest of the city, and the beginning of an important process of conversion to Christianism by many Jews who moved to Christian quarters where no Jew had ever dwelt before.

Prior to this date, the Jews lived to the north of the city, around Puerta Osario, Campo de la Merced and Santa Marina quarters.

So, according to all the evidence we have, the commercial, artisan and administrative ecclesiastical centres were still situated, in Christian times as in former times, around the Mosque, proclaimed a Cathedral Church after the conquest, and situated not far from the Christian monarchs' Alcázar (LO 112). Ramírez de Arellano quotes in *Paseos,* n. 959, several testimonies from the XIII and XIV centuries that confirm the existence of this Jewish quarter in the place indicated above.

CHAPTER X

THE CORDOBA SYNAGOGUE

We do not know how many synagogues existed in the aljama (or Jewish quarter) in Christian Córdoba after the city's conquest by Ferdinand III.

What is certain is that the one preserved today was not the only one. From a papal bull issued by Innocence IV (1250) we know that,' in mid XIII century, shortly after Ferdinand III conquered the city in 1236, a protest was made by the ecclesiastical archdean and chapter in Córdoba because of the «excessive height» of a synagogue being built. In this bull the Bishop of the diocese was instructed to take the appropriate measures with respect to the synagogue under construction which was causing «grave scandal to devote Christians and detriment to the Córdoba Church», breaking the law in force at that time on monuments of this type.

The text of the bull reads as follows: «Innocentius episcopus, servus servorum Dei, Venerabili fratri episcopo Cordubensi salutem et apostolicam benedictionem. Contra inhibitionem dilectorum filiorum Archidiaconi et capituli Cordubensium, sicut accepimus, judei Cordubensis civitatis quamdam synagogam superflue altitudinis temere ibidem construere de novo presumunt, in grave Christi fidelium scandalum et Cordubensis ecclesie detrimentum. Quare humiliter petebatur a nobis ut provide super hoc misericorditer curaremus. Qua cura fraternitati tue per apostolica scripta mandamus quatinus contra judeos eosdem super hoc officii tui debitum, cessante apellacionis obstaculo, exequaris. Dat. Lugduni idus aprilis, pontificatus nostri anno septimo», (RB 241).

Some authors, like Castejón (among others), believe the remains of this great synagogue can be seen in the house in Maimónides Square, ancient (Papal) Bulls Square, very near the present synagogue, with

133

beautiful patios and formerly rich in carved panels, today the Municipal Taurine Museum, and which some guides to Cordoba refer to as «Maimónides' house». However this opinion has no textual or archaeological evidence to support it (CB 5). Others, like Fita, quoting Amador de los Ríos (*Historia,* I, 556-557) maintain that the «site (of this synagogue), an oblong rectangle... and its disproportionate height match the building (of excessive height) that in 1250 the Hebrews in Córdoba wanted to erect, meeting with the opposition of Innocence IV» («Noticias», *BRAH* V [1884] 201).

We believe the endeavour to build a synagogue of large dimensions on the part of Córdoba Jews does not so much obey the desire for revenge or for coming out on top, as has sometimes been suggested, but follows their custom of choosing the highest point of the city to build their synagogue in obedience to the Babilonian Talmud (Tos Meg 4,22-23), and if this were not possible, that they should try to make the building higher than the surrounding ones. The Babilonian Talmud says: «Any city whose roofs are higher than the synagogue will eventually be destroyed» (BT Šab 11a). When this could not be put into practice, in the Middle Ages the custom was to erect a pole or mast on the synagogue's roof that would stand out above the neighbouring buildings.

THE CORDOBA SYNAGOGUE. HISTORY OF A MONUMENT

The Córdoba synagogue was built around 1315 (by the Jewish calendar year 5075 which commenced 20th September 1314 and ended 1st September 1315).

SANTA QUITERIA HERMITAGE AND HYDROPHOBIA HOSPITAL

After the expulsion of the Jews in 1492 the synagogue was dedicated as a hermitage to Santa Quiteria, and the house was turned into a hospital for hydrophobic patients.

CRUZ DE CRISTO AND SAINTS CRISPIN
AND CRISPINIANO HERMITAGE

In 1536 a confraternity called Cruz de Cristo y San Crispín was installed in the synagogue; it underwent reformation, passing to the shoemakers' guild (fraternity) in April 1581 with the name of Saints Crispín and Crispiniano. This association used the place for its chapter meetings and patron feasts. In a document «it is recorded that Bishop Don Francisco Pacheco approved the Confraternity of the said Saints, conferring statutes to this guild on 8th June 1588, and that the Church of the aforesaid Hermitage was "of old the Jewish synagogue that the Hebrews maintained in this Capital as the Construction shows, being as they are all the walls of the said Church full of Hebrew inscriptions"» (cf. *Bulas, Privilegios, Ordenamientos reales del Rey Don Juan II y otras escrituras sacadas de los Archivos... de Córdoba*, Volume XVI, part III, conserved in the library of the Royal Academy of History, C.16, case 25, shelf 1a; page 676; quoted by CB 5, n.4; also FF 397).

This guild used it during the whole of the XVII century, a fact confirmed by a quotation from Sánchez de Feria in 1722, whereby «the inscriptions that remained had been damaged and from lack of interest were now obliterated with modern repairs». So a restoration took place around 1722 or at least repairs were carried out to the damaged parts in detriment to the inscriptions that had been there since it was built (SG 66).

According to Fita (p. 398), Feria only speaks «of the inscriptions in the places that were subjected to repairs badly understood and carried out even worse by people who had no idea of the epigraphs' value. These were obliterated, that is, partly destroyed and partly whitewashed with a thick coat of lime. But that did not prevent there being *at the top part* of the said church all four walls full of Hebrew inscriptions».

It is not to be wondered that Don Pedro de Madrazo neither in his *Recuerdos y bellezas de España* (with illustrations by Parcerisa), nor in his volume on *Córdoba*, I of *España, sus monumentos y artes* (Barcelona 1884), makes no mention whatsoever of the synagogue (CB 6, n.5).

And Santos Gener comments (p.66): «When, by order of the

Governor, Venegas and Domínguez inspect papers in the local archives, in the one at St. Crispín (in whose building he states there are Hebrew inscriptions) a document is found dated 1794 in which the Shoemakers' Guild requests that a quota be set to raise funds to repair the roofs of the vault which were falling into ruin. From this text it seems apparent that at this time the roof was repaired and the vault was constructed which would hide the Mudéjar plasterwork from view during the XIX century, until in 1880 Padre Párraga discovered the inscriptions when part of the western wall peeled, and these were studied by Padre Fita. The synagogue had fallen into such a state of forgetfulness on the part of scholars of the time, because of the erection of the aforesaid vault and the daubing of the walls, that the meticulous Don Luis Ramírez de las Casas Deza failed to include the synagogue (perhaps he did not know of its existence) among the notable monuments of Córdoba in the catalogue the Monuments' Commission charged him to draw up for the Governor, and Amador de los Ríos himself says nothing at all about the inscriptions in his work *Historia,* I, 369.»

This vault — of reed and plaster — that began just at the height where the arch starts on the western wall, to the left of the entrance door to the prayer hall, hid most of the synagogue's plasterwork as well as the Hebrew inscriptions until they were discovered by P. Párraga.

According to Cantera (p. 6) this was the most important modification that the synagogue underwent throughout its history, that is, «the substitution, at the end of the eighteenth century, of the old carved ceiling by a reed vault, because by 1794 the roofs of the original vault were falling into decay». The vault, which caused serious harm to the synagogue's highest double epigraphical frieze, in 1751 did not yet exist, as can be seen from a document taken from the Guild's confraternity's *Libro de los acuerdos desde 1787 a 1815.* It reads: «In the City of Córdoba, *tenth of March Seventeen Ninety Four,* the members of the Shoemakers' Guild... meeting together in the St. Crispín and St. Crispiniano Martyrs' Hermitage, in which they are accustomed to celebrate their community events, and by virtue of the summons they have received, proceeded before me, the undersigned Public Scribe, collegiate and fellow of the said

136

City and Mayor of Royal revenues of the city and its kingdom, to celebrate council, in which the following was dealt with.»

«In this Council the Senior fellow of the said Hermitage and Governors Francisco Lladosa and Miguel Berjel reported the urgency and necessity to repair and mend *the roof of this Hermitage's vault,* which threatens total ruin that could cause considerable damage, and perhaps injury, resulting *from having parted in the centre the Main beam, which supports all the Structure of the roof.* And to avoid such imminent risk, confirmed by different inspections made, and instance on the part of various Master Builders, who have shown contextually the said need and danger, with special recommendation and warning having been made that to delay would increase the risk; this is made manifest to the Guild, so that, its members being aware, they may take a decision in this matter, and with corresponding haste do what they consider most convenient and correct; conceiving that, according to the opinion of the said Master Builders nothing can serve as a remedy, unless it be the *execution of the said work».*

«And having heard the whole Guild the aforesaid proposal, and taking into consideration that its funds cannot cover at the moment the cost that the said construction work would involve, and at the same time the urgent need and warning not to delay, it was agreed to effect a General distribution among all the members of the said Guild, to cover the whole amount that the said work occasions» (FF 398-399).

The synagogue, converted into a church, is described in the following terms by Ramírez de Arellano (p. 573, No. 948): «...The church is small, square and extremely damp; in the vestry the priests hardly have room to robe themselves for the title service, the only service celebrated during the year: it has two altars, the first on the Gospel's side, where it was transferred by the new fraternity; it supports the ancient sculptures of Santa Quiteria and Saint Bartolomé; on the main altar is a Conception, and on each side St. Crispín and St. Crispiniano and above, a crucifix, all of little value; the same as St. Peter and St. Paul painted as frescos on the wall: both altar pieces are poor, painted blue with gilt. Over the vestry door there is a picture, representing the Triumph or monument dedicated to St. Raphael next to the bridge gate, and beside it the full portraits of Charles IV, his wife and Ferdinand VII, whose awful portraits were painted to celebrate the arrival of the three in Córdoba, which were put up in the street with a ridiculous sonnet, all dedicated by the Shoemakers' Guild, and afterwards installed here in memoriam...»

NATIONAL MONUMENT

The Córdoba synagogue began to recover something of its original appearance in 1884 when the chaplain, Don Mariano Párraga, discovered the beautiful plasterwork on the walls when part of the plaster covering the western wall fell away.

On 31st October 1884 the Royal History Academy was asked to declare the synagogue a national monument (*BRAH* V [1884] 400). This is the text of the application: «The signatories have the honour of proposing to the Academy their approval of the declaration as a national monument the Córdoba synagogue, constructed in 1315 by Hebrew craftsmen with absolute religious exquisiteness and beauty. Its emplacement, its select and numerous inscriptions of the best caligraphical type, its incipient Mudéjar style, origin of the flowery and sumptuous style that reigns in the famous *Tránsito Synagogue* in Toledo, and finally, the interest that it has begun to excite among learned persons, whose aspirations would be frustrated if a monument of such great historical and artistic value were left to a quirk of fate in a moment of upheaval; these are the reasons we submit to the Academy's criterium and consideration, trusting they will consider them with their accustomed wisdom. Signed Francisco de Cárdenas, Francisco Fernández González, Fidel Fita. Madrid, 31st October 1884.»

A year later, in 1885, it was declared a national monument, and its period of restoration commenced.

This same bulletin in 1884 (pp. 201-203, with photo) presents a fragment of the inscription which Fidel Fita recovered from the debris and presented to the Academy, from 1 Cr 16:28 with the word *(m)išpehot,* a word from the verse that says: «Give unto the Lord, ye kindreds ([m]išpehot). Give unto the Lord glory and ([m]išpehot) strength», a verse that also appears in the Tránsito Synagogue (Toledo), elaborated under the patronage of King Don Pedro, and embellishes the top part

138

of the southern wall. In this report from BRAH the Royal Academy is promised «it will shortly receive drawings of the rest, made by Don Rafael Romero, our correspondent in Córdoba, author of the first descriptive report on this arquitectonic monument, no less worthy of conservation and being attended in its restoration than the Santa María la Blanca and Tránsito synagogues in Toledo...» (Romero Barros was the first director of the Museo Provincial de Bellas Artes in Córdoba; his study titled «La Sinagoga de Córdoba» is signed 15th January 1878 and published in *BRAH* V [1884] 234-264). However, in the same bulletin, Fita (p. 267), on receiving a copy of the inscription sent by Romero Barros, states that the inscription quoted is not from 1 Cr 16:28 but from Psalm 22:27: «All the ends of the world shall remember and turn unto the Lord: And all the kindred *([m]išpehot)* shall worship before thee», as on the lower line on the western wall are the first four words of this Psalm and the first letter of the next. The rest are missing; but some fragments remain, lying on the floor of that side of the vault; with the exception of the piece Fidel Fita picked up in the little garden close by and brought to the Academy.

CHRONOLOGY OF SUCCESSIVE RESTORATIONS

In order to establish the chronology of the synagogue's successive restorations, we shall follow Santos Gener very closely (pp. 66-67).

— 1886.   Report by the provincial architect Don Rafael Luque to the Monuments' Commission on the collapse of a porch roof which existed in the entrance patio, 4 metres long and 1.20 wide of which, at the moment when the report was made, only the supporting bridge remained, snapped, and the railing hanging, with no materials remaining from the part collapsed. Quotation for the repair work: 150 pesetas.

— 1898.   Don Enrique Romero de Torres writes an article in the *Diario Córdoba* newspaper on 20th November denouncing the state of the synagogue. The State grants 4.000 pesetas and entrusts the restoration to the architect Don Joaquín Fernández Casanova.

— 1899.   The approved restoration was not carried out; on 19th July, the General Direction of Fine Arts requests the Provincial Monuments' Commission to report on Don Fernando Casanova's restoration project.

— 1900. An elemental restoration must have been carried out under the supervision of Don Mariano González Rojas, who came from Seville under delegation in Señor Casanova's name. The remaining altars were removed «various niches were filled in», the plasterwork was uncovered and *tiled work* that decorates the walls, recovering its primitive character and appearance. (Señor Romero Barros' actual words are between commas.) So it was on this occasion that the baroque vault was removed (*BRAC* XIV [1935] 398).

In 1904, Ramírez de Arellano (*Inventario,* p. 133) comments on the restoration in the following terms: «The altars were dismounted and later, in 1900, the plaster and lime vault was removed and a new ceiling made and the walls were repaired; furthermore, an ignorant bricklayer, off his own bat, completed the plasterwork in a luckless show of good will.» And on page 135 he describes the synagogue in these terms: «The site of the miserable building is almost square. The entrance is through a flimsy modern door over which there is a sort of gallery with three balconies onto the temple, decorated with small ornamental arches with minute stucco work... The decorative elements are almost the same as the ones in the Enrique de Trastamara chapel in the Cathedral, but crudely done, with lines that get lost or stray from the geometrical pattern they should follow. To be brief, it is very poor compared to what was done almost at the same time in Granada and a little later in Córdoba and Seville. This does not mean, however, that it should not be conserved and restored in a more serious way than it has been to date, bearing in mind it is one of the few synagogues we have left and also the period in which it was inaugurated.»

— 1916. During this year proceedings were taken to transfer the St. Crispín and St. Crispiniano Hermitage, formerly the synagogue, to the Córdoba Provincial Historical and Artistic Monuments' Commission. Indeed, as is recorded in a document dated 25.3.1916 — I have been able to study the photocopy in the file on the synagogue in the Regional Andalusian Government's Cultural Council Delegation in Córdoba — the Governor, President Agustín de la Serna, applies to the ecclesiastical authorities for the transfer of the St. Crispín and St. Crispiniano Hermitage, formerly synagogue, to the Córdoba Provincial Historical and Artistic Monuments' Commission, putting forward as an argument in favour of this

140

transfer that «the famous Tránsito and Santa María la Blanca synagogues were also transferred to the Toledo Commission». By the Governor's request, on 25th March 1916, the parish priest of the Sagrario applied to the Pope's Apostolic Ambassador in Spain for the monument's transfer to this commission, and this application was countersigned by Ramón, Bishop of Córdoba, on 29th March 1916, giving, among other reasons, that of «worship is no longer held in this place, which is of limited dimensions, that little benefit can be gained by the Church from retaining it, being in constant risk of having to spend larger sums of money and, finally, to put an end to the dicussions that have lasted for eighteen years between the Public Instruction Ministry and Fine Arts and the Ecclesiastical authorities».

On 3rd April 1916, the Pope's ambassador, Don Francisco Ragonesi, gave the corresponding authorization for its transfer and, on 19th April, the Bishop of the diocese wrote the decree of transference delegating in the Sagrario Parish Priest as ecclesiastical administrator to «hand over and give possession of the same to the referred Commission in the person or persons he saw fit to name» (this document, dated 8th May, was sent to the Civil Governor and to the Sagrario ecclesiastical administrator).

The person delegated in, named by the Commission, is Don Enrique Romero de Torres, secretary to the Córdoba Provincial Historical and Artistic Monuments' Commission. The Governor, President Agustín de la Serna sends a letter on 16th May 1916, thanking the Bishop for the transference, acknowledging receipt of the Bishop's notification of 8th May that same year. Finally, on 8th June 1916, in the Córdoba synagogue in the presence on the one part of Don Antonio Rodríguez Pinar, Chancel Rector and Ecclesiastical Administrator, Sagrario parish priest representing the Bishop and, on the other part, of Don Enrique Romero de Torres, representing the Córdoba Provincial Historical and Artistic Monuments' Commission, the aforesaid monument was handed over and taken possession of, together with all its outbuildings.

— 1919. The Monuments' Commission applies for state aid to undertake its full restoration (especially because of the bad state of the ceiling).

— 1920. 7th April. A request is made to the General Direction of Fine Arts to command Señor Velázquez Bosco to design the project he was commissioned to do in July and which, according to Santos Gener «if it had been done, should be filed in the Public Instruction Ministry».

— 1928. The Governor, Don Antonio Almagro Mendes manages to get the General Director of Fine Arts, Señor Conde de las Infantas, to raise a sum for restoration. This action prepared the ground, according to Cantera (p. 6), for the definitive repairs, outlined in a project of which Santos Gener's publication is a documentary report. Local architects are named: Enrique Tienda Pesquero, provincial architect; Carlos Sáenz Santa María de los Ríos, municipal architect; and as the archaeologist apointed for the said Commission, the Director of the Archaelogical Museum, Don Samuel de los Santos Gener, who for this occasion wrote a lengthy report on the possibilities for the restoration, dated November 1928 and published in *Anales de la Comisión de Monumentos Históricos y Artísticos de Córdoba,* 1927-28 (pp. 65-81) with the title «La Sinagoga de Córdoba».

RESTORATION BY DON FELIX HERNANDEZ JIMENEZ

The restoration was undertaken in 1929, being entrusted this time to the architect Don Félix Hernández Jiménez.

«On inspecting the ceiling and poor framework that existed at that moment, the base of the pilasters of the high windows was discovered, which means reconstructing the arches and lifting the ceiling to its original level, confectioning a simple loop framework to evoke the one that must have existed before. This gives greater sumptuosity to the temple, which appeared stunted. This time the restorer eliminated the plasterwork that had been renewed during the former restoration, leaving only the ones considered original and substituting the supposed renovations with plain panels» («Miscelánea», *BRAC* XIV [1935] 398-399). The southern wall was restored to its original state in the same way, removing the two arches resting on columns in the centre, leaving the entrance door in the centre of the south wall, as it remains today. Thus restored the synagogue has remained to this day. This restoration was technically guided by Don Félix Hernández with special care, although, according to Cantera (p. 6) he may perhaps have been too drastic in certain aspects, for example, with the inscriptions. This author comments, in this respect (p. 16): «It is a pity that the latest restoration of the synagogue, with its drastic elimination of the legends (without the prudential advice of persons with a deep knowledge of the Hebrew language) has left the walls bereft of a large part of the inscriptions that decorated them up until that moment — as is the case of the inscription on the south wall.»

It will be necessary in the future to make a detailed study of the criteria used for this restoration, as well as all intervention in the matter of the inscriptions.

THE LATEST INTERVENTION IN THE SYNAGOGUE AND CUSTODIAN DWELLING

— 1977. On 28th February the architect Carlos Luca de Tena y Alvear informs the Córdoba Historic and Artistic Patrimony Commission of the «bad condition it (the synagogue) is in, almost in ruins and, because of the storms in Córdoba in the last months, falling into a dangerous state. It is necessary — according to the architect's report — to undertake the reconstruction of the roof, substituting its frame, and to repair or substitute all the woodwork and provide drainage for the ground floor, as the lack of foundations causes serious damp in all the walls».

In April the same year the said architect presents «the estimate for repairs to the porter's dwelling within the synagogue building» to reform the dwelling which was also in a sad state, at a total cost of 193,881.40 pesetas.

— 1981. On 4th March the Provincial Delegation for the Ministry of Culture in Córdoba wrote to the architect Don Joaquín Serrano Díaz in these terms:

«On 25th February the General Subdirection for Artistic Patrimony informed us that you have been commissioned to design a project for the restoration of the synagogue», with a total cost of 5,000,000 pesetas.

I beg you to confirm your acceptance of this commission, and, at the same time as I urge you to carry it out with the utmost celerity, I take the liberty of advising you to transmit the said project through this Provincial Delegation, so that the Provincial Commission for Historic and Artistic Patrimony have knowledge of it. Yours faithfully, Provincial Delegate: M. Nieto».

On 29th September 1981 the *Diario Córdoba* reports on the meeting held in the town of El Carpio by the Provincial Commission for Historic and Artistic Patrimony, approving the project for the synagogue's restoration and «recommending the monument's restoration programme be extended to include the commission of a project related to the plasterwork, for the Conservation and Restoration of Works of Art Institute».

— 1983. 21st September, the *Diario Córdoba,* in its local section, in a report signed by R. L., announces «a contract coming up to public offer for a project, designed by the architect Joaquín Serrano Díaz, to restore the synagogue in Córdoba and its adjoining rooms for a total cost of 5,083,936 pesetas to be invested by the Ministry of Culture's Subdirection for Artistic Patrimony to repair the worst of the damage observed in this historical building constructed in 1315 as well as the guard's dwelling, particularly affected by the damp and passage of time. In this way the Provincial Direction will see an old desire fulfilled, as this project was commissioned in 1981, although the work has not been given the green light until now, and it would probably begin in November, with the precinct closed while work is going on... The most serious damage appreciated is to the temple's roofing, as, owing to its bad state, water filters in, with damp appearing in the beams and timberwork of the roof structure as well as in several places inside, especially where the ceiling comes to rest on the upper gallery. All this means that there is a risk that the damp may cause irreversable damage to the Mudéjar plasterwork that decorates the inner side of the walls. The rest of the deterioration affects different elements: walls presumably in bad condition, mortar revetments that are cracked, mouldy or coming away, very deteriorated woodwork, and paintings that have deteriorated or are non-existent... Furthermore, according to the report on the mentioned project, apart from technical and construction problems presented by the bad state of the building, and because of the scarce living quarters available, serious problems have been posed of a practical nature in order to endow the adjoining dwelling with a minimum of conditions, which at the same time endeavour to provide openings for sufficient ventilation and light to make it inhabitable. Finally, we must say that as far as the construction work is concerned, the general idea of the project on the point of seeing the light is to respect the materials and formal characteristics of the existing building. To this end, beams and roof-frame will be restored, conserving at the same time the dwelling's ironwork. The roofing of the upper gallery and its stairs will also be reconstructed with suitably treated boards and logs, whilst the existing ballustrade and wooden elements will be respected. In this way, taking special care to match new materials with old ones, the elegance of one of Córdoba's most ancient and venerable buildings will be recovered, and all who today wish to delve into Córdoba's millenary roots will be able to visit it.»

In the end the construction work was granted to Francisco Rodríguez Cívico's firm, to «reform the synagogue and adjoining rooms» according to file «No. 1256 (1983-1988), Judios Street» in the Regional Andalusian Government's Cultural Council Delegation in Córdoba. Earlier (26.10.83), this construction work had been granted to Construcciones Labrador Gómez, S.A., being rescinded later for not having presented the necessary papers. The estimate for the work, according to the *Diario Córdoba* on 20.9.83 was 5,083,936 pesetas and, according to the file 19.6.86 it was 4,997,509 pesetas.

— 1984. 23rd June. In an article also signed by R. L., the closure of the synagogue to the public was announced, in order to carry out its restoration, for approximately 120 days, at an estimated 4,997,509 pesetas. In this newspaper the report given by the same author on 21st September 1983 was repeated and the specific actions were summarized as: eliminate leaks and damp existing in the inner facing of the temple. The constructive solutions proposed (making good of walls, revetments, new roofing and remaking cornice) guarantee total elimination of the problem, according to the experts, and other actions would complete the work (substitution and repair of woodwork, paintwork, etc.) in order to attain an adequate state of conservation for the whole building.

As far as the adjoining quarters are concerned, the present project resolves, within the limited space, the programme of basic necessities for the guard's dwelling, providing kitchen and bathroom, minimal, but sufficient according to the terms of the project...

After the construction work, the synagogue was opened once more to the public during Maimónides' week (25-30 March 1985), commencement of the celebration of the 850th anniversary of Maimónides' birth. On this occasion a numerous group of Jewish personalities from different countries celebrated a religious service in the Synagogue.

CHAPTER XI

TWO VISITS TO THE CORDOBA SYNAGOGUE

1. DETAILED VISIT *

Number 20, Judíos (Jews) Street, in the Judería (Jewish Quarter), between the Almodóvar Gate and the *Bab al Yahūd* (Jews Gate) to the north, and Maimónides Square, formerly (Papal) Bulls Square, to the south — a large wooden door opens onto the patio before the Córdoba synagogue. High up on the left of the door, in tiles: The Synagogue.

The Córdoba synagogue is «one of the most historic and attractive synagogues in the whole world» (CB 3). It is the purest of the three mediaeval synagogues conserved in Spain, as its basic architectural structure has never been affected by adaptations; it is the only mediaeval synagogue conserved in Andalusia.

THE ENTRANCE PATIO

Once through the door and down two steps we enter the patio before the synagogue. This patio had a porch roof 4 metres long by 1.20 wide with an iron railing. This roof collapsed before 1886, as Santos Gener (p. 68) says that «today only the bridge that supported it remains standing, snapped, and the iron railing, hanging, with no materials at all remaining from the part collapsed».

As is the custom among Jews and according to what the Babylonian Talmud in the *Běrakot* (8a) tractate sets down, that a syna-

---

* See complete photografic coverage of the Córdoba synagogue at the end of this edition.

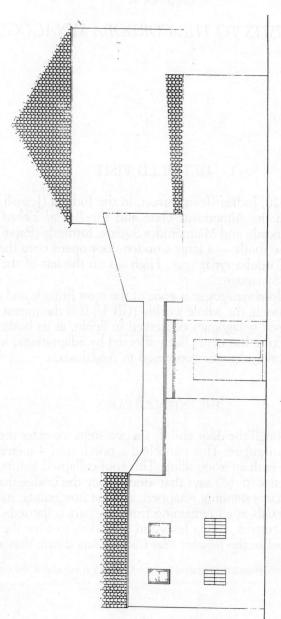

Front perspective of the Córdoba synagogue. Latest restoration. Architect: Joaquín Serrano

gogue should not be entered directly from the street, the entrance is by way of a tiny patio of 5.80 by 4.25 ms. This space between the street and the prayer hall should be used — as Juda Loew Bezalel from Praga explains — to «leave worldly thoughts and worries outside before entering the sacred sanctuary». The patio, like the typical patios in Córdoba houses, is full of pot plants, very clean and well looked after, the same as the rest of the precinct.

Mediaeval synagogues used to have a basin for the Jews' hand (and foot) ablutions. We do not know if the Córdoba synagogue had one, but we do know that water was plentiful in the place from a well — covered today — in the right hand corner of the tiny patio before the guard's house, on the left of the synagogue's patio. This well was used until a few years ago when running water was installed in the guard's house, and its mouth was almost completely covered over. We also have evidence of wells in buildings adjoining the synagogue on the western and northern outside walls. We do not know if these wells existed in the Middle Ages to supply the mediaeval synagogue with water, as we understand no archaeological research has been carried out at the bottom of them. In any case, the winding street, coming down from north to south, leads us to believe that, the same as in other similar streets in the city, under its surface subterranean water is to be found at no great depth. The need for water for synagogue services was so evident that, in not a few cases throughout history, they were built close by rivers or on the beach (p. 52).

Opposite the entrance door to the synagogue patio a marble plaque commemorates the 800th anniversary of Maimónides' birth in Córdoba. It reads:

VIII Centenary of Maimónides
1135 — 30 March — 1935

SPAIN, FROM THE NATION'S GOVERNMENT,
EXPRESSES ITS HOMAGE
TO THE IMMORTAL GENIUS OF JUDAISM

CORDOBA, HIS HOME,
HONOURS HIS MEMORY

A similar plaque, in ceramic, was placed in 1985 in the Tiberiades Square, by Maimónides' statue, to commemorate the 850th anniversary of the birth of this illustrious polygraph, celebrated throughout 1985 with different cultural and scientific events. The programme of the various acts has been compiled in an appendix to the Spanish edition of the book *The Jews in Córdoba (X-XII)*, number 3 of the series *Estudios de Cultura Hebrea*.

THE CUSTODIAN'S DWELLING

On the left of the patio a small door with an iron screen opens onto the little patio before the modest dwelling where the Pérez family lives; the members of this family, grandfather, son and grandson, have taken care of this monument since 1945. On the left of this tiny patio there is a sink for laundry and a small bathroom and, on the right, the well, covered today, and a small room or larder under the stairs. On the ground floor there is a living room and a kitchen with windows looking out onto the street; on the first floor two little bedrooms also with outside windows.

This dwelling, in Cantera's opinion (p. 7), «could be basically coetaneous to the synagogue, the same as the other cottages that enclose it to the west and north. In the dwelling on the side that separates the synagogue from the city wall — opposite the patio entrance door — and even more in the one on the north side — to the right — Mudéjar arches, plasterwork and pieces coetaneous to the synagogue have been discovered, and it was in these dwellings that the synagogue's adjoining offices must have been, for example

150

the *madrisa* or Talmudical school, small meeting rooms or the Hebrew aljama etc.». And this author comments: «We can only add that, after having examined the mentioned dwelling, in the part adjoining the city wall, where a stilted arch leads out to the

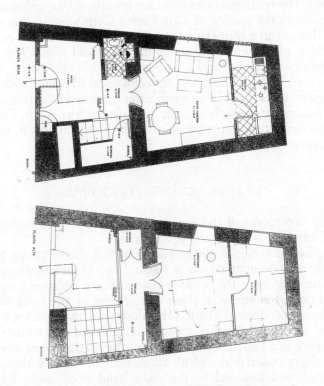

Plan of ground and first floors of dwelling adjoining the synagogue. Latest restoration. Architect: Joaquín Serrano

country, we have observed an ample room, on the walls of which there still last pairs of arches which start at floor level and go more than half way up various of the walls, with voussoirs in alternating earth and brick. These could be considered as remains of one of

151

the synagogue's rooms.» Earlier (1928) Romero Barros (p. 70), referring to the houses adjoining the synagogue, wrote: «For four centuries the aforesaid houses, occupied by families, have undergone such modifications in their patterns and structures that almost nothing original remains that could lead us to consider their reconstruction. The remaining elements are limited to two columns and three bases in the garden of Don Carlos Ortiz's house that could have belonged to a Mudéjar portico, and the beginning of an arch of Mudéjar plasterwork still set in the foral wall with a few small fragments of the same, and a wooden epigraphical "aluer" which is conserved in the Provincial Archaeological Museum with such scarce elements we feel it impossible to recommend the restoration of the *madrisa* and much less the capitular aljama room, but just limit the reconstruction work to the hall of worship itself, that is, the Synagogue.»

THE SYNAGOGUE'S ENTRANCE HALL

Only two rooms of the synagogue itself have been conserved: a small entrance hall and the prayer hall.

On the right of the synagogue's patio is the entrance to the vestibule, the door of which is flanked by two windows, with a third one overhead: the windows we can see today are not the original ones, but traces of these can be seen on the same wall to the left of the door (CB 5). (The door and the windows were replaced during the latest restoration to substitute the former ones which were in a bad state and were not the original ones anyway.)

On the occasion of the 850th anniversary of Maimónides' birth, a *mĕzuzah* was fastened to the right hand door jamb, halfway up. The *mĕzuzah* is a metal box containing a piece of parchment on which the text of Dt 6:4-9 and 11:13-21 is written in 22 lines (p. 64). On the back of the *mĕzuzah* is written the Hebrew letter *shin,* the first letter of the principal Jewish prayer, the *Šema'* (p. 78).

Both the door to the entrance hall and to the prayer hall are on the south side of the building and not on the east or west as was usual in ancient Palestinian synagogues (p. 55). The advantage

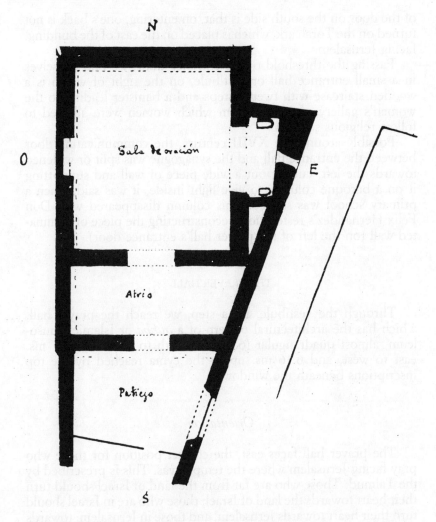

Layout of synagogue's entrance and prayer hall (reproduced from F. Cantera's book: Las sinagogas españolas, *page 9)*

of the door on the south side is that, on entering, one's back is not turned on the Torah ark, which is placed on the east of the building, facing Jerusalem.

Passing the threshold of the entrance door, we find ourselves in a small entrance hall or vestibule, on the right of which is a wooden staircase with twenty steps and a banister leading to the women's gallery, the place from which women were allowed to follow religious services.

Possibly around the XVIII century, the communicating door between the entrance hall and the synagogue was split or widened towards the left, cutting out a wide piece of wall and supporting it on a baroque column, to give light inside, it was said, when a primary school was started. This column disappeared with Don Félix Hernández's restoration, reconstructing the piece of eliminated wall (on the left of the prayer hall's entrance door).

THE PRAYER HALL

Through the vestibule, up a step, we reach the prayer hall, which has the architectural pattern of a *qubba* or Islamic mausoleum, almost quadrangular (6.95 ms. north to south by 6.37 ms. east to west, and 6.16 ms. up to the cyma reached by the top inscriptions beneath the windows).

Orientation

The prayer hall faces east, the correct position for those who pray facing Jerusalem where the temple was. This is prescribed by the Talmud: Those who are far from the land of Israel should turn their heart towards the land of Israel; those who are in Israel should turn their heart towards Jerusalem, and those in Jerusalem, towards the temple... So those to the north of Jerusalem turn to face the south; those in the south, to the north; those in the west, to the east, in this way all Israel prays (facing) towards the same place (Tos Ber 3,15-16; p. 54).

154

*Transversal perspective of the synagogue's entrance and prayer hall.
Latest restoration. Architect: Joaquín Serrano*

Decoration

a) *Plasterwork*

The first thing to notice on entering the prayer hall is that the four walls are covered with plaster decoration.

Light enters through five windows opened on the north wall (opposite the entrance door), another five on the south wall (the side of the door) and another five on the west wall (on the left when entering), three of which are filled in, giving a total of twelve round arches or windows between the ceiling and the decoration for light to enter the room. The synagogue should have plenty of light (Š Ar OH 90,4) and, therefore, windows. The Talmud forbids praying in a room without windows (TB Ber 34b) and the *hălakah* establishes that the synagogue should have twelve windows, one for each of the tribes of Israel, although this has rarely been carried out literally (p. 57). Curiously, the Córdoba synagogue has twelve open windows as, of the fifteen round arches or windows, three are filled in.

Nothing remains of the original ceiling; it has been replaced with a modern structure of dowelled angle rafters and experts suspect it should have carved panels.

Between the floor and the plasterwork, the stonework of the walls can be seen, as their original revetment has disappeared; restorers have not been able to discover if it once had a tiled wainscoting, plasterwork down to the floor, or some other solution.

According to «Miscelánea» in *BRAC* XIV (1935) 398, «it has a high wainscoting, bare today, that might have supported rich tiling or tiled mosaics, that have completely disappeared, but must have matched the splendid example almost wholly conserved today in the neighbouring XIII century monument, called the Saint Bartholomew chapel, which guards the building of the «Hospital de Agudos», today Faculty of Arts.

The plaster decoration on the walls can be classified, in style and composition, in two areas: the eastern wall (to the right of the entrance door), clearly different to the rest, and the other three walls which present a high degree of uniformity.

The *eastern wall* (on the right of the entrance door) is the most important, as here is where the chamber is opened to keep the

Law scrolls. The revetment decorating this niche has been badly damaged; only the top part of the panel remains, patterned with diamonds full of plaster vegetation with a small pineapple in the centre of each. The border is a Hebrew epigraphical frieze. It is likely that, originally, the lower part terminated in three small arches on little columns, like the eastern wall of the *Tránsito* synagogue in Toledo, very similar to our Córdoba one. On each side of the chamber a carved panel with large stars completes the decoration and, underneath, Hebrew inscriptions of four lines (the one on the left has disappeared).

Inside the opening 2.80 ms. wide that contained the *'aron* (ark that contained the Torah scrolls) there are two niches, apparently coetaneous to the synagogue. The one on the right, 1.12 ms. above the floor, is 0.54 ms. deep by 1.50 ms. high by 0.43 ms. wide; the one on the left is set into the wall and is about 2 ms. high and 0.65 ms. wide, sitting 0.76 ms. above the floor of the chamber. Between them signs can be seen of a sort of window frame that in the XIV century gave onto the street, mistakenly considered by Romero Barros as the synagogue entrance (RB 255; cf. CB 17). Above the chamber opening, high up, there is an elegant frieze of 18 small arches with the Arab expression, stretched out, *baraka li-llah:* «Blessed be the Lord»; these little arches are similar to the ones on the high windows in the Tránsito synagogue, frequently found decorating Arab and Mudéjar doorways. Unfortunately, everything that existed between this point and the ceiling has been lost, probably disappearing when the original ceiling fell in (CB 20).

The walls *on the north* (opposite the door), *on the west* (on the left) and *south* (wall with the entrance door) are united by a decorative frieze at the top, bordered along the top and bottom edges with a line of Hebrew inscriptions with another decorative frieze at the bottom, interrupted on the west wall — to the left of the entrance door — by a niche and on the south by the entrance door. The principal motif of both decorations is a geometrical pattern, based on fine lines crossing to form stars, on a background of vegetation. At some unknown date the south wall (where the entrance door is) lost the upper line of writing, while the lower line suffered modifications, adding vertical epigraphical bands on each end and bordering the openings for the windows.

157

Between the two friezes, from a symmetrical central axis, the space on each wall has been divided into three parts: a central panel and two side ones, separated from each other by panels with geometrical and floral patterns.

Symmetry is lent to the whole on the *north wall* (opposite the entrance door) by a graffito imitation of the windows that give onto the women's gallery.

There are similar imitation windows on the *west wall* (on the left of the entrance door), the centre of which is occupied by a panel decorated with an ornamental diamond pattern and closed at the bottom with a small pointed arch with lobes, matching the decoration on the east wall. Inside, where the arch begins, are two plaster plaques, both the same, decorated with digited ferules and other vegetation and geometrical motifs of clear Almohade origin (XIV century).

In each of them, under arches, the word *al-mulk* can be read twice and at the top the end of the word *baraka* with obvious signs of restoration.

The right hand plaque is in better condition than the one on the left, although both are perfectly legible.

The beginning of the inscription must have read: الملك لله (*al-mulk li-llāh*) which can be translated as «power is God's» or «power belongs to God». This inscription is the sign left everywhere by Mudéjar artists on monumental decoration.

> This phrase has often been incorrectly translated as «Jehovah, all reign and power». Thus Fita (p. 391) followed by Cantera (p. 29) for whom the Arab inscription reflects the «Davidical meaning» of Psalm 22:29.

It is quite likely that this arch and its niche 43 cms. deep contained the *bimah* or platform for Torah readings and directing religious services. The *bimah* in mediaeval synagogues used to be on the opposite side to the ark, on the west side of the chamber. We know what it was like from miniatures in XIII century manuscripts. Inside the arch is a cross, painted in black and red, which could be from the end of the fifteenth or from the sixteenth century. In the XVI century an altarpiece of Santa Quiteria was placed here when the synagogue became a hermitage.

On the *southern wall,* with the entrance door, is the women's gallery or tribune that communicates with the prayer hall by way of three small balconies. Above them is a wide decorative frieze more than half a metre wide and a line of inscription that has totally disappeared, and five windows.

b) *The Hebrew inscriptions*

Completing the decoration on the synagogue's walls is a series of inscriptions — mainly taken from the Book of Psalms — in square Hebrew characters, originally in flesh colour on a blue background, according to Fita (p. 399, n.1) who collected the epigraphical fragments found lying on the floor in order to take them to the city's archaeological museum. «Some of them, says this author, show at the broken edges that the letters were flesh coloured and stood out on a blue background.» The letters are about 9 to 10 cms. high.

> We shall give the English version of the Hebrew inscriptions, line by line, so the reader can see the translation of each of the lines of the text that appears on the walls. We shall put in bold type only the part of the English text that corresponds to the Hebrew still conserved on the wall. When an original Hebrew word is incomplete, we shall use bold type for the letters or words that correspond to the English word. In this way the reader can obtain an idea of the fragmentary state of the text conserved, and at the same time, understand the whole of the original text, lost today. For readers versed in Hebrew we shall transcribe the Hebrew inscription at the foot of the page, following Cantera Burgos' version and indicating the text lost today within brackets.

EAST WALL

On the right of the entrance door to the prayer hall is the eastern wall. In the centre of it there is a chamber 2.80 ms. wide, in which the *'aron,* ark or cupboard, was placed containing the Torah scrolls (the Pentateuch or the five first books of the Bible) and the *Haftarah* (Prophet's writings) which were read and commented at religious services (p. 57).

On the right of this chamber there is a Hebrew inscription 1.19 ms. long by 55 cms. wide, whose text refers to the founder of the synagogue, Yiṣḥaq Moḥeb, and to the date of its construction. It reads (written from right to left) *:

**Provisional sanctuary and abode for the Testimony
completed by Yiṣḥaq Moḥeb, son of Mr. Efraim
Wadawa, in the year seventy five. So return,
Oh God hasten to return to Jerusalem!**

We have preferred to translate the Hebrew expression *miqdaš me'at* for «provisional sanctuary», and not as «small, modest or tiny sanctuary» as is usually done, as this expression does not refer to the modest size of the synagogue. As Cantera so rightly states (p. 22): «it should not be taken literally as "small or modest sanctuary" in the sense that another one existed, or that the building of a larger one would not have been permitted as some have thought». The expression *miqdaš me'at* is taken from the book of the prophet Ezekiel (11:16) which reads: «Therefore say, Thus saith the Lord God; Although I have cast them far off among the heathen, and although I have scattered them among the countries, yet will I be to them as a little sanctuary (*miqdaš me'at*) in the countries where they shall come.» The prophet Jeremiah refers to the exile in which the people, bereft of the Jerusalem temple, turn to God who in punishment has sent them far from their land; but God has not gone right away from his people. Out in the desert He provides them with a reduced presence, a sort of minor sanctuary; lacking in temple and worship, they had the law, the priests and the prophetic word. The expression *miqdaš me'at* is applied to synagogues in the Middle Ages to indicate their provisional

----

* מקדש מעט ונוה תעודה שכללו
יצחק מתב בן הגביר אפרים
ודוה שנת שבעים וחמש כן שעה
[ה]אֵל וחיש לבנות ירושלם

160

nature in contrast to the permanent character of the Jerusalem temple whose reconstruction was anxiously awaited. It was considered that the synagogue's functions as a sanctuary were justified whilst the Jerusalem temple was constructed; in this sense they are temporary or provisional buildings.

«Moheb», the surname of the synagogue's founder, is a word related to Arab *Muḥibb*, «friend, lover». The Mohib, Moheb or Mohep surname has appeared frequently in Toledo and its territory (Maqueda, etc.) since the first half of the thirteenth century, being documented also the name of Yiṣḥaq Moheb in the same period as our Córdoba inscription (CB 23).

The date — year 75 — is to be taken as the year 5075 by the Jewish calendar that commenced 20th September 1314 and finalized 1st September 1315.

On the left of the chamber set in this wall, matching the inscription commented, must have been another which has been totally lost.

The arch that surrounds this chamber is framed by an epigraphical border whose text almost entirely disappeared in the penultimate restoration; the three lines were almost completely conserved in 1928 when Santos Gener wrote his report on the Córdoba synagogue. The text is written from the bottom upwards, starting out on the right side of the arch, going round the top and down the left side. It reads.*:

— right side (from bottom upwards) (Psalm 138:2):
I will worship toward thy holy temple, and praise **thy name:** *For thy loving kindness and for thy truth, for thou hast magni -*

---

*   אשתחוה אל היכל קדשך ואודה את] שמך עָל חסדך ועל
אמתך כי הגדל]ת על כל שמך אמרתך: אחת שא]לתי מאת יְיָ
אותה] אבקֵ֥שׁ שבתִּ֫י בן]בית יְיָ כל ימי חיי לחזות בנעם יְיָ
ולבקר בהיכלו].

— top (right to left) (Ps 138:2; 27:4):
fied thy word above all thy name. One thing have I de*sired*
of the Lord, that will I
— left side (from top downwards) (Ps 27:4):
seek after; *That I may dw***ell in** *the house of the Lord all the*
days of my life, to behold the beauty of the Lord, and to
enquire in his temple.

NORTH WALL

The north wall (opposite the entrance door to the prayer hall)
culminates in five round arches through which light enters the
prayer hall. Under the arches there are two lines of inscriptions
that run from right to left and continue along the west wall (on
the left of the entrance) and on the south (wall with the entrance
door). They are texts from Psalms 95:6; 132:7; 99:5; 100:1b.2a;
86:9 and 95:1 (top line) and 29:2; 96:9; 66:4 and 22:27,28 (bottom
line).

What can be read there, translated into English, is the following:
— top line *, north wall (from right to left: Ps 95:6; 132:7
and 99:5). The inscription is almost wholly conserved:
O come, let us wor*ship and b***ow down: Let us kneel (?) be-**
fore the Lord, our maker / We will go into his tabernacles:
We will **wor***ship at his* **fo***otstool / Exalt ye the Lord our*
God, and worship at his footstool; for **he** *is holy.*
— top line, west and south walls (from right to left: Ps
100:1b.2a / 86:9 / 95:1). Only some words can be read:
Serve the **Lord with gladness: Come before his presence**

---

* בואו נש]תחוה ונכר]עה נכררה לפני י'י עושנו נבואה
למשכנותיו " נש]תחוה לה]דם רנליו: רומו י'י אלהינו
והשתחוו להדום רנליו קדוש]וא [עבדו את] י'י בשמחה בואו
לפניו [ברננה כל נוים] אשר עש]ית יבואו וישתחוו
לפניך י'י ויכבדו לשמך לכו נרננה לי'י נריעה לצור ישׁע]נו:

with singing / All nations [**whom thou hast** *ma]de shall come and worship before thee, Oh Lord; and shall glorify thy name* / *Oh come let us sing unto the Lord: Let us make a joyful noise to the rock of our sal***vation.**

In this text the expression **whom thou hast ma***de* inexplicably appears in the middle of the line underneath and not on the top line where it corresponds.

— Bottom line * on north wall (from right to left: Ps 29:2 / 96:9 — cf. 1 Chr 16:29,30 — / 66:4). Almost completely conserved:

Give **unto the Lord the glory due unto his name; Worship the Lord in the beauty of holiness** / *Fe***ar before him, all the earth** / **All the earth shall worship thee, and shall sing unto thee; They shall sing to thy name. Selah.**

— bottom line of west wall (from right to left: Ps 22:27.28). Most of the text is missing:

All the ends of the earth **shall remember and turn unto the Lord:** *And all* **the kindred** *of the nations shall worship before thee. For the kingdom is the Lord's: And he is the governor among the nations.*

This lower line on the west wall, as we have said, has the phrase *whom thou hast ma*de, which belongs to the upper line.

_____

* ‏[הב]ו ליֵיֵ כבוד שמו השתחוו ליֵיֵ בהדרת קדש:השתחוו‎
‏ליֵיֵ בהדרו נלוש יֵיֵ [ח]ילו מלפניו כל הארץ:כל הארץ ישתחוו‎
‏לך ויזמרו לך יזמרו שמך סלה ‖ : יזכרו וישובו אל יֵיֵ [כל‎
‏אפסי ארץ וישתחוו לפניך כל הַשפחות [גוים כי ליֵיֵ המלוכה‎
‏ומשל בגוים].‎

Attracting our attention on the western wall (to the left of the entrance door) is a splendid ogival arch whose sides measure 1.52 ms., crowned with a panel of rhomboidal plasterwork patterns. The Hebrew inscription that frames it seems to refer to the Song of Songs (4:4).

Santos Gener, in his article, reproduces two photographs of the successive state of this wall: one, prior to 1900 when the decorative part of the wall was covered by a vault and another, when the article was written (approx. 1928). It is deplorable that today almost the entire lower line of the inscription has disappeared as well as the inscription surrounding the arch, both of which appear to be well conserved in the 1928 photo.

But let us take a closer look at the inscription that surrounds the arch today:

— right side (from bottom upwards) *
A series of Hebrew letters, whose meaning cannot be deciphered: **wšmšnyy hqšṭ bnwy ltlpywt.**
— top (from right to left) **:
A rosette with six petals followed by the phrase: **I am builded like the tower of the Messiah, Lord...** This sentence is not a literal quotation from the Song of Songs, but is similar to one quoted by Fita «Thy neck is like the tower of David builded for an armoury, whereon there hang a thousand bucklers, all shields of mighty men» (Song 4:4). This is what Fita read from the inscription (p. 386) but it is not the verse that appears today nor the one in the photo taken in 1928, quoted by Santos Gener.

— left side (top to bottom) ***:
Fragments of three words remain **pny pny... bwrḥw...**

---

*   ושמשניי הקשט בנוי לתלפיות

**   אני בנוי כמגדל, משיח אל...

*** ..פני פני.... בורחו..

The inscriptions on this western wall are completed by the Arabic inscription inside the beginning of the ogival arch, which we have commented when describing the plasterwork (p. 158).

SOUTH WALL

For the following commentary on the inscriptions on the southern wall we must bear in mind the general appearance of the synagogue's interior southern wall, whose picture we reproduce from F. Cantera Burgos' book, *Sinagogas españolas* p.11.

On this wall, the inscriptions are in a sad state, especially the lower part, as a section of this wall (left side on entering) was replaced by two arches resting on a central column. These arches and columns were eliminated in Don Félix Hernández's restoration, recovering their former appearance.

In the centre of this wall is the doorway to the prayer hall. This doorway measures 1.80 ms. wide by 3.10 high. Above the door is the women's gallery (2.75 ms. wide) with three small balconies surrounded by partially conserved Hebrew inscriptions. The decoration is completed by four rectangular panels with plasterwork half-way up, as far as the beginning of each of the arches. The top half of each section has a panel of sixteen decorative loops, matching the top frieze (SG quoted by CB 12). Above these balconies is a wide ornamental frieze, which culminated in a horizontal band of writing along the whole wall, completely absent today.

1. The inscription that frames the wall itself (vertical line on the extreme right and left of the wall) comes from Psalms 84:1-3 and 13:6:

— Vertical line on right end of wall (from bottom upwards: Psalm 84:1-3, terminating in a rosette) *:

מה ידידות משכנותיך א' צבאות : נכספה וגם [כלתה נפשי לחצרות *

י"י לבי ובשרי ירנני אל אל חי]

165

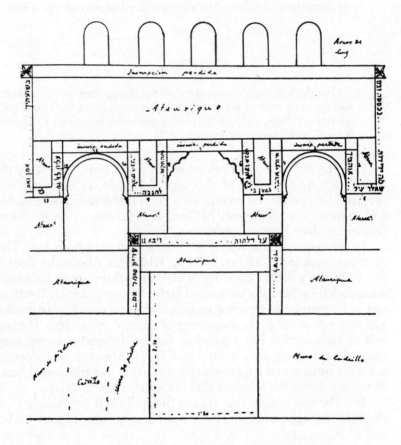

Arcos de ciey

Inscripción perdida

Ataurique

inscrip. ondida   inscrip. perdida   inscrip. perdida

עַל דַּלְתוֹת . . . . וַיָּבֹא

Ataurique

Ataurique   Ataurique

Muro de ladrillo

Castillo

General appearance of south wall inside the Córdoba synagogue (Reproduced from F. Cantera's book, Sinagogas españolas, *page 11)*

How amiable are thy tabernacles, O Lord of hosts! *My soul* **longeth,** *yea even fainteth for the courts of the Lord: My heart and my flesh crieth out for the living God.*

— Vertical line on left end of wall (from top downwards: Psalm 13:5-6, commencing with a rosette) *:

But I have trusted in thy mercy; My heart shall rejoice **in thy salvation. I will sing unto the Lord, because he hath dealt bountifully with me. Amen and Amen.** And this is all we can read today. According to Cantera (p. 16): «Between these verses, traces of which still remain on the wall... there was still in line — judging by the southern frontal wall — a space in which could well have fitted one of the psaltery verses: Ps 26:8: *Lord, I have loved the habitation of thy house, and the place where thine honour dwelleth.* Or Ps 61:4: *I will abide in thy tabernacle for ever: I will trust in the covert of thy wings.*

2.   The inscriptions that frame the windows or balconies are in a very sad state today, to such a point that we can hardly trace but a few words or odd letters and unintelligible parts of others. The first inscription that can be read, commencing on a line with the beginning of the arch over the right hand balcony and reading from right to left as in a maze, until we reach the horizontal line over the central balcony, comes from Psalm 122, verses 6-9 **:

Pray for the peace of Jerusalem: they shall prosper that love thee. *Peace be within thy walls, and prosperity within thy palaces. For my brethren and companions' sakes, I will now say, Peace be within thee. Because of the house of the Lord our God I will seek thy good.*

---

* ‏[ואני בחסדך בטחתי יגל לבי] בישועתיך"אשירה ליʼʼי כי גמל‎
‏עלי: אמן ואמן :‎

** ‏שאלו של[ום] ירושלם ישליו אוהביך [יהי שלום בחילך -‎
‏שלוה בארמנותיך למען אחי ורעי אדברה נא שלום לך :למען‎
‏בית ייʼ אלהינו אבקשה טוב לך:‎

167

Our efforts to indicate the text remaining on the wall in bold type are defeated as from verse 6 («Pray for the peace of Jerusalem: they shall prosper that love thee») which is fairly well conserved; verse 7 has completely disappeared; «confused parts of letters and words» remain from verse 8; from verse 9 «remains of about seven letters and three complete words followed by others blurred today, with a Hebrew word 'bqš which appears to be the beginning of the verse of another Psalm reproduced in the second part of the arrab» (CB 14).

The inscription continues down the left side of the central balcony as far as the end of the wall towards the left going round the balconies. Cantera proposes as plausible readings Psalm 102: 12-13 and Ps 57:2-3. Psalm 102 reads:

But thou, O Lord, shalt endure for ever; And thy remembrance unto all generations (v. 13 totally disappeared). *Thou shalt arise, and have mercy upon Zion: for the time is come to favour her, yea, the set time is come* (v. 14 blurred traces of which remain, followed by the text of Psalm 57:2-3). This is the text of Psalm 57:1-3: *Be merciful unto me, O God, be merciful unto me: for my soul trusteth in thee: Yea, in the shadow of thy wings will I make my refuge, Until these calamities be overpast. I will cry unto God most high; Unto God that performeth all things for me* (scattered letters and the odd complete word remain of this text).

3. The inscription that frames the entrance door *:

— right side (bottom upwards, terminating in a rosette: Prov 8:34 and Is 26:2):
Blessed is the man that heareth me, **watching**

— top part (right to left, terminating in a rosette): *da***ily at my gates, waiting at the posts of my doors / Open ye the gates, that the righteous nation may enter in**

— left side (top downwards):
which keepeth the *truth.*

---

* [אשרי אדם שמע ל]י לשקד .על דלתת]י יום י]ום לשמר מזוזת פתחי:
פתחו שערים ויבא גו[י] צדיק שומר אמ̇ונים]

168

Inside the women's gallery

The women's gallery — not visitable today — is situated over the entrance hall and communicates with the prayer hall, as we have just seen, by way of three small balconies. A window on the south side of the gallery gives onto the synagogue's patio. The gallery is 2.75 ms. wide. On its western and southern walls and also on the floor, fragments of plasterwork, inscriptions and some archaeological pieces as well as fragments from small columns can still be found today, as in a tiny museum. Among the remains of inscriptions three fragments are of special interest, corresponding to the words from Psalms 96:8 and 95:1, which were originally on the top line of the inscription on the western wall.

* * *

THE SYNAGOGUE TURNED HERMITAGE

We cannot conclude this chapter dedicated to a detailed visit of the Córdoba synagogue without describing its appearance during the period it was used as a Catholic Hermitage. In order to do so we shall closely follow the description by R. Romero Barros in his article «The Córdoba Synagogue», BRAH (1884) 234-264.

Over the wall with the entrance door to the synagogue's patio stood «a rough bell tower, sword shaped».

The synagogue's entrance hall was separated from the prayer hall «by a thick wall parallel to the entrance wall, perforated by two arches of the same height and shape that led to the tiny church». The entrance hall was whitewashed and had «an enormous picture in the centre of which a pious sonnet was written in huge letters, as much lacking in correction and sense as full of faith and Catholic enthusiasm». Ramírez de Arellano (p. 573, No. 948) situates this picture over the sacristy door, that is, on the eastern wall. The picture, according to this author, represented «the Triumph or monument dedicated to St. Raphael next to the bridge gate, and beside it the full portraits of Charles IV, his wife and Ferdinand VII, whose awful portraits were painted to celebrate the

169

arrival of the three in Córdoba, which were put up in the street with a burlesque of a sonnet, all dedicated by the Shoemakers' Guild, and afterwards installed here in memoriam...».

The prayer hall was covered with a «heavy Greek-Roman vault that disfigured its original shape». This vault covered the Mudéjar decoration we can see today.

The Hermitage's presbytery was on the north wall, opposite the entrance door, with a gilt altar panel and some sculptures. Ramírez de Arellano (p. 537, No. 948) describes the two altars in the Hermitage: «The original one on the same side as the Gospel — west wall — moved there by the new brotherhood: supports ancient sculptures of Saints Quiteria and Bartholomew»; on this wall the first traces of the ancient construction were found. On the plasterwork panels on this wall were "a St. Cristopher and a Rosary virgin, painted in oils with energetic frankness and not a little skill and intelligence"»; on the high altar — north wall — is a Conception, and on either side St. Crispín and St. Crispiniano and a cross overhead, all of little value; the same as the St. Peter and St. Paul painted as frescos on the wall; both altar panels are poor, wooden, painted blue with gilt details». Romero Barros is of the same opinion and refers to «St. Peter and St. Paul, rough and completely repainted; and in the corners, other panels of a different kind but no less disagreeable decoration...»

In the east wall's chamber (to the right of the entrance door), «a square door gives onto an irregular narrow space destined, it seems, to keep the sacred ornaments». On this wall was «an oil painting, whose high degree of mutilation and deterioration prevents us from judging its worth; (this painting) for many a long year covered the surface of this large space...» This is the wall where Romero Barros mistakenly places the synagogue's main door.

The synagogue's ceiling is described by Romero Barros in these terms: «we can only add to the chamber formed by the four walls we have described, the crown, a rough ceiling of thick beams and timbers which produces a disagreeable effect and which not long ago, undoubtedly, replaced the precious delicately worked panels? that watched over it in its better years.

170

2. BRIEF VISIT

Synagogue — in Hebrew *bet ha-kĕneset* — is a word that comes from Greek *synagôgê* and means «meeting». The synagogue is the Jews' meeting or meeting place.

According to the most commonly accepted opinion, the synagogue originated in Babylonia, during the Jews' exile (587 B.C.), and was consolidated as such on their return to Palestine (536 B.C.).

THE JEWS IN CORDOBA

We do not know the exact date as from which nuclei of Jews have lived in Spain. The first epigraphical evidence that is absolutely reliable is of a family, of Palestinian origin, inhabitants of Hispania, which goes back to the second century of our era.

But it would be in the X-XII centuries when Spanish Judaism would enjoy a real renaissance, reaching its golden age here, in Córdoba, the capital of al-Andalus or Moslem Spain. The Jewish influence in Córdoba declined at the end of the Caliphal period, but recovered when, conquered by Ferdinand III, an edict was issued according equal treatment to Christians, Moslems and Jews, at least in theory.

THE CORDOBA SYNAGOGUE

At number 20 Judíos (Jews) Street, just a few metres from the Tiberiades square, where Maimónides' monument stands, is «one of the most historic and attractive synagogues in the world».

The Córdoba synagogue was built in 1315 (5075 by the Jewish calendar). This was certainly not the only synagogue in the aljama or Jewish quarter.

After the Jews' expulsion from Spain in 1492, the present synagogue was dedicated as a Hermitage to Santa Quiteria and the house as a hydrophobic hospital. In 1588 it was transferred to the brotherhood of the shoemakers guild under the patronage of Saint Crispín and Saint Crispiniano, and would be used for the brother-

171

hood's acts and patron feasts. In the XVIII century the plasterwork ceiling was replaced by a cane and plaster vault, because the ceilings in the original vault were caving in. A priest, Don Mariano Párraga, when part of the plaster came away, discovered the plasterwork on the walls in 1884. A year later, in 1885, it was declared a national monument, and its period of restoration commenced.

As is the custom among the Jews, the synagogue is not entered directly from the street, but by way of a small patio. On the right of it is the entrance door; to the left, the dwelling for the synagogue's custodian.

The synagogue has two rooms: a small vestibule and the prayer hall itself.

Crossing the threshold of the entrance door, we find ourselves in a narrow *vestibule,* on the right of which is a flight of stairs that lead up to the women's gallery, from where they were allowed to follow religious services.

By way of the vestibule, up a step, we reach the *prayer hall* which is almost quadrangular (6.95 ms. north to south by 6.37 ms. east to west, and 6.16 ms. high, up to the cyma reached by the top inscription beneath the windows). The lower part of the walls has lost its original decoration, but the richness of the Mudéjar plasterwork on the top part — a fine example of how the Jews used the Mudéjar craftsmen for their construction — gives an idea of the original beauty of this building. The synagogue's decoration is composed of plasterwork panels (decorative plaster relief peculiar to Arab art) forming stars of four, six or eight points, mingled with vegetation motifs in Morisque style. This decoration on the walls is completed by a series of inscriptions — mostly taken from the book of Psalms — in square letters 9 to 10 cms. high, originally flesh coloured on a blue background.

On the right of the entrance door to the prayer hall is the *east wall.* In the centre is a chamber 2.80 ms. wide, in which the *'aron* was placed (ark or cupboard containing the Torah scrolls, that is, the first five books of the Bible or the Pentateuch). Inside this chamber, on right and left, there are two niches or cupboards, apparently coetaneous to the Synagogue. By the tabernacle chamber, on the right, an inscription 1.19 ms. long by 55 cms. wide has

172

been conserved. Its text refers to the synagogue's founder, Yiṣhaq Moheb, and reads: «Provisional sanctuary and abode for the Testimony completed by Yiṣhaq Moheb, son of Mr. Efraim Wadawa, in the year seventy five. So return, Oh God hasten to return to Jerusalem!»

The *north wall* (opposite the prayer hall's entrance door) is covered in the same paneled plasterwork crowned by five round arches through which light enters. Beneath the arches there are two lines of inscriptions running from right to left and continuing along the west wall (to the left of the entrance) and along the south (wall with the entrance door). The inscriptions are verses from Psalms 95, 132, 99, 100, 86 and 95 (the top one) and 29, 96, 66 and 22 (the lower one).

On the *west wall,* to the left of the entrance door, there is a splendid ogival arch whose side measures 1.52 ms. and it is crowned with a panel of rhomboidal plasterwork patterns. The Hebrew inscription that frames it, almost completely lost, seems to refer to the Song of Songs (4:4). This ogival arch and its niche 43 cms. deep must have held the *bimah* or pulpit for Torah readings. In the centre of the niche is a cross painted in black and red, which could be from the late fifteenth or from the sixteenth century; this was where the altar panel to Santa Quiteria was placed when the synagogue was converted into a hermitage.

On the *south wall,* over the entrance door, is the women's gallery or tribune, which communicates with the prayer hall by way of three small balconies, framed by partially conserved Hebrew inscriptions. Over them is a decorative frieze more than half a metre wide; above it, a line of inscriptions totally lost today, and five windows. The inscriptions on this wall are from the books of Proverbs, Isaiah and Psalms.

We can say little about the offices adjoining the main hall that all synagogues used to have. In the houses adjoining the synagogue's west wall, some arches and remains of an ancient building have been discovered that might well have belonged to these adjoining offices, lost today.

173

SELECTED BIBLIOGRAPHY

PART I
THE SYNAGOGUE

AVI-YONAH, M., «Sinagogas Antiguas en Israel», in *Ariel* 26 (1973) 29-44.
BONSIRVEN, J., *Textes rabbiniques des deux premiers siècles chrétiens,* Roma 1955.
KRAUS, S., *Synagogale Altertümer,* 1922.
LEVY, I., *The Synagogue: Its History and Function,* London 1963.
LÖW, L., «Der synagogale Ritus», in «Gesammelte Schriften» IV (1898) 1-71.
MEYERS, E. M., *Synagogue,* in *IDBS* (1976) 842-844.
NAVARRO PEIRÓ, A., *La literatura hispanohebrea (siglos X-XIII),* Córdoba 1988.
PELÁEZ DEL ROSAL, J., *Los orígenes del pueblo hebreo.* Second edition, Córdoba 1988.
— (ed.), *Para entender a los judíos,* Córdoba 1984.
— (ed.), *Los judíos en Córdoba* (siglos X-XII). Second edition, Córdoba 1988.
SÁENZ-BADILLOS, A. / TARGARONA BORRÁS, J., *Poetas Hebreos de al-Andalus (siglos X-XII). Antología,* Córdoba 1988.
SAFRAI, S./STERN, M. (ed.), *The Jewish People in the first Century (Compendia rerum Judaicarum ad Novum Testamentum)* I, Amsterdam 1976, pp. 908-945.
SIGONIUS, C., *De republica Hebraeorum libri VII,* 1583.
SCHÜRER, E., *Historia del pueblo judío en tiempos de Jesús,* 2 vols., Madrid 1985.
SONNE, I., *Synagogue,* in *IDB* IV (1962) 476-491.
STRACK, H. L./BILLERBEECK, P., *Kommentar zum Neuen Testament aus Talmud und Midrash,* vol. IV, München 1928, 115-188.
SUKENIK, E. L., *Ancient Synagogues in Palestine and Greece,* London 1934.
— «The Present State of Ancient Synagogue Studies», in *Bulletin of the L. M. Rabinowitz Fund for Exploration of Ancient Synagogues* 1 (1949) 8-23.
Synagogue, in *Enc. Jud.* 15 (1971) cols. 579-84; 591-602.
VITRINGA, C. V., *De synagoga vetere libri tres,* 1696.

WATZINGER, C., *Antike Synagogen in Galilaea,* 1920.

WEINGREEN, J., «The Origin of the Synagogue», in *Hermathema* 98 (1964) 68-84.

PART II

THE CORDOBA SYNAGOGUE

AMADOR DE LOS RÍOS, J., *Historia social, política y religiosa de los judíos de España y Portugal,* Madrid 1973.

CB: CANTERA BURGOS, F., *Sinagogas españolas,* Madrid 1955 (reprint 1984).

CARO BAROJA, J., *Los judíos en la España Moderna y Contemporánea,* 3 vols., Madrid 1962.

CASTEJÓN Y MARTÍNEZ DE ARIZALA, R., «Córdoba califal», *BRAC* 25 (1929) 255-339.

EC: ESCOBAR CAMACHO, J. M., *La ciudad de Córdoba en la baja Edad Media. Aproximación a su estudio desde el punto de vista urbanístico.* Doctoral Thesis, 2 vols., Faculty of Arts, Department of Mediaeval History, Córdoba 1987, pp. 665, 21 plans y 31 graphs.

— «La creación del Concejo de Córdoba a través de su Fuero», *BRAC* 103 (1982) 131-138.

FF: FITA, F., «La sinagoga de Córdoba», *BRAH* V (1884) 361-399.

— «La sinagoga de Córdoba, monumento nacional», *BRAH* V (1884) 400.

— «Noticias», *BRAH* V (1884) 201-203.

— «Informes», *BRAH* V (1884) 267-268.

GRACIA BOIX, R., «El Corral de los Ballesteros», *BRAC* 90 (1970) 5-24.

GONZÁLEZ JIMÉNEZ, M., *En torno a los orígenes de Andalucía: La Repoblación del siglo XIII,* Publicaciones de la Universidad de Sevilla 1980.

LEVY PROVENÇAL, E., *Historia de España,* vols. IV-V, España musulmana, pp. 711-1031, Madrid 1982.

LO: LÓPEZ ONTIVEROS, A., *Evolución urbana de Córdoba y de los pueblos campiñeses,* Diputación Provincial de Córdoba 1981 (Second edition, with corrections and additions).

MADRAZO, P. de, *Córdoba,* Barcelona 1980.

— *España. Sus monumentos y artes —su naturaleza e historia—* Córdoba, Barcelona 1886.

MATEOS, J./CAMACHO, F., *El horizonte humano. La propuesta de Jesús,* Córdoba 1988.

NEUMAN, A. A., *The Jews in Spain,* I-II, Philadelphia 1969.

NIETO CUMPLIDO, M./LUCA DE TENA, C., «El Alcázar Viejo, una repoblación cordobesa del siglo XIV», *Axerquía* 1 (1980) 231-273.

ORTI BELMONTE, M. A., «El fuero de Córdoba y las clases sociales en la ciudad. Mudéjares y judíos en la Edad Media», *BRAC* 70 (1954) 5-94.

— *Córdoba monumental, artística e histórica,* Diputación Provincial de Córdoba 1980.

RAMÍREZ DE ARELLANO, T., *Inventario monumental y artístico de la provincia de Córdoba,* Diputación Provincial de Córdoba 1904.

— *Paseos por Córdoba,* Córdoba-León 1936/1976.

RAMÍREZ DE ARELLANO Y DÍAZ DE MORALES, R., *Inventario-Catálogo histórico artístico de Córdoba,* with notes by J. Valverde, Córdoba 1983.

RAMÍREZ Y DE LAS CASAS-DEZA, L. M., *Indicador cordobés. Manual histórico topográfico de la ciudad de Córdoba,* León 1948.

RB: ROMERO BARROS, R., «La Sinagoga de Córdoba, hoy ermita dedicada al culto bajo la advocación de San Crispín», *BRAH* V (1884) 234-264.

SG: SANTOS GENER, S. DE LOS, «La sinagoga de Córdoba», *Anales de la Comisión Provincial de Monumentos Históricos y Artísticos de Córdoba* (1927-1928) 65-85.

TORRES BALBÁS, L., «Estructura de las ciudades hispanomusulmanas: la medina, los arrabales y los barrios», *Al-Andalus* 18 (1953) 149-177.

Entrance door to the Córdoba synagogue in Calle Judíos, 20 (20 Jews' Street)
(photo by Huedo)

Entrance door to the dwelling adjacent to the synagogue (photo by F. González)

Synagogue patio. On the right, the entrance to the vestibule. Far end, plaque (1935) commemorating the 800th Anniversary of Maimonides' birth in Córdoba (photo by F. González)

Córdoba synagogue: vestibule. (photo by F. González)

Córdoba synagogue: Eastern wall (photo by Huedo)

Córdoba synagogue: Northern wall (photo by Huedo)

Córdoba synagogue: Western wall (photo by Huedo)

Appearance of the Western wall with the beginnings of the dome which hid the plasterwork (Santos Gener, page 66)

Southern wall. Women's gallery (photo by Huedo)

*Southern wall
prior to Félix
Hernández's
restoration*

Interior of the women's gallery (photo by F. González)

Córdoba synagogue: Eastern and Southern walls (left to right on photo)
(photo by F. González)

View of the synagogue from the women's gallery (photo by F. González)

GLOSSARY

ʿĀbodah (work, service). Sacrificial cult in the synagogue. Later, this term would come to be refer to prayer, like «ʿābodad from the heart».

Aljama. (From Aram ȳamāʿa, group of persons; ȳamāʿat al yahūd, group of Jews.) Aljama is the name for the district where Jews lived within the territorial area corresponding to the Castille Crown. The aljama was also equivalent to council and had its communities or jurisdictions and, in them, always subordinate to the municipalty, other «torahs» or quarters. The equivalent Hebrew word is →qahal.

Al-mimbar. →Al-Memar.

Al-memar. Distorted form of Aram al-mimbar used to refer to the platform or pulpit from which synagogue services were led. →bimah.

Almojarife. Tax collectors in the →aljama. Later collectors of all royal taxes and, very often, the King's treasurer.

ʿĂmidah (prayer «standing up»). Basic prayer at all religious services; so called because it was said while standing.

Amoraim (expounders). Jewish teachers from the period following the →Mishna (250-420 A.C.)

Anathema. Religious institution in Israel which consisted of consecrating for extermination, on religious grounds, people, animals and objects. →Herem.

Aramaean. Western Semitic language, very similar to →Hebrew, spoken from the end of the second millenium by seminomads who invade the Fertile Crescent. Aramaean displaced Hebrew as the Jewish people's vernacular language from 586 B.C. (fall of Jerusalem) and the Babylonian exile.

Ark of the Covenant or Torah. Wooden box containing, apparently, the Law tables on which the decalogue was inscribed (Dt 10:1ff; 1 Kgs 8:9). It was deposited in the Holy of Holies in Solomon's temple and covered with gold plate, the mercy seat (Ex 25:17-21) or →kapporet (originally «to cover sins»; later «to take away sins»). The mercy seat was a gold placque, decorated with two cherubims, seat of divine presence and place of Yahve's

177

pardon by the High Priest sprinking sacrificial blood on Expiation day (→*Yom Kippur*).

ʾǍron ha-qodeš. Wooden box in whcih the →*Torah* scrolls were kept. →*Ark of the Covenant.*

Av, Nine days of. Commemoration of the Temple's destruction.

Baraitot (excluded). When the Mishna, recopilation or legal code of earlier halakite laws was put into writing, those halakite rules not included in the Mishna were called *baraitot*. Later, much of this material omitted by the Mishna came to form part of the →*Talmud*. The *baraitot* also contains →*Haggadah* elements.

Bet ha-kěneset. House of meeting. →*Synagogue.*

Bet ha-těfillah. House of prayer. →*Synagogue.*

Bet ha-midraš. House of study. Study is one of the →*synagogue's* three functions; the other two are prayer and assembly.

Bimah. Pulpit or platform from which →*synagogue* religious service was led. →*Al-mimbar.*

Cabala (interpretation). Mystic interpretation of the Scripture practised in certain Jewish and Christian circles in the Middle Ages, also astrological and witchcraft practices based on this interpretation. Its classical work is the *Zohar.*

Canaan. Name for Palestine before the arrival of the Hebrews.

Covenant. Symbol taken from international political relations (feudatory pacts) or from nomadic customs (blood alliances) used in the Scriptures to describe the relationship between God and men. The Covenant Code is a set of different types of laws and can be found in Ex 20:22-23:19.

Decalogue. The ten commandments that form the clauses of the Sinai →*Covenant* (Ex 20:1-17; Dt 5:6-21).

Deraš (research or study). Rabbinical interpretation of the Bible that endeavours to discover the hidden meaning of the text.

ʾEtrog. The cedar which, together with the palm or →*lulaḥ,* makes up the ceremonila branch used at the →*Sukkot* feast to declare the sanctification of these feast days.

Gemara' (complement). Commentary on the →*Mishna* by Palestinian and Babylonian Rabbis that, together with the Mishna would later form part of the→*Talmud*. It includes discussions by the Sura and Pombedite Academies on the search for the biblical sources behind the laws contained in the Mishna in order to extract new laws for cases not anticipated. It was written by the →Amoraites. The *Gemara'* is not a code but a faithful reproduction of the academies' discussions.

Gĕnizah (from Aram *gnz,* to be precious, to be hidden). Chambers in the →synagogue in which Jews were obliged to deposit the manuscripts of the sacred book no longer fit for liturgical use. These would be buried after a certain time in holy ground, being preserved meanwhile from all possible profanation or corruption.

Hafṭarah (conclusion or dismissal). Bible readings from the Prophets which, according to some, concluded synagogue services. The prophets were read after the →*Torah* and the latter was completed by them according to the expression in use, like *hifṭir bĕ-nabi:* dismiss (the community) with the prophets (TP Sanh 1,19a).

Haggadah (announce, tell). Jewish interpretation of the Scripture with an exhortatory tendency, using edifying prose. This term was used to refer to the parts of the →Talmud that are not strictly jurisdicial and religious, but are used for teaching and educating. The *haggadah* is parallel to the →*hălakah,* and is frequently used to support its regulations.

Hălakah. (Derived from *halak* «to march, walk, proceed».) Jewish interpretation of the Scripture with the aim of deducing ethical and jurisdicial regulations for the «procedure» or conduct of an individual or of the community. The most strictly legal part of the →*Talmud* is referred to with this term. The *hălakah* is parallel to the *haggadah,* and is of a rather edifying nature.

Hănukkah. Feast of lights or temple dedication.

Hazzan. (Derived from *hazzah,* «to see», giving *hazzan,* «watchful». The *hazzan* is a servant to the →synagogue or sacristan under the authority of the *roš ha-kĕneset* or head of the →*synagogue.*

Hebrew. Western Semitic language in which most of the Old Testament was written. Very similar to →*Aramaean,* it was displaced by this living language from the Babylonian exile, remaining, nonetheless, as a literary or academic language.

Heḳal (temple). Among Sephardies it is used to refer to the place or shrine in the →synagogue where the ark containing the →*Torah* scrolls is placed.

Ḥerem. Expulsion from the community of one of its members. Equivalent to biblical →*anathema.*

Kaddiš (sanctification). Doxology recited at synagogue services by the mourners in memory of those deported.

Kahal. Jewish quarter. →*Aljama.*

179

Kidduš (sanctification). Prayer of blessing sung to God over the goblet of wine on the Sabbath and feast days, declaring the keeping of these holy days.

Lulaḇ. The palm in the form of a ceremonial branch for the →*Sukkot* feast service, together with leaves of myrtle, willow and →*'etrog* or cedar.

Ma'āmad (position). Synagogue service coinciding with the turn of levites and priests on duty in the temple. →*Mišmar.*

Madrisa. Name given in the Jewish world to the Talmudical school. →*Bet ha-midraš.*

Mĕgillah. «Volume or roll», because of the form of ancient books, made up of various pieces of papyrus, sewn together one after the other, so that, once each end had been fixed to rods or cylinders, they could be rolled round them, especially when the rolls were bulky (cf. Is 34:4; Zech 5:1ff; Ps 40:8). Five form the *Mĕgillot* or volumes that are read in the →synagogue throughout the liturgical year: Song of Songs (at Passover), Ruth (at Pentecost), Lamentations (on the ninth day of the month of Av, commemorating the destruction of the temple), Ecclesiastes (at the feast of Tabernacles) and Esther (feast of →*Purim*). The *Mĕgillah* tractate of the →Mishna contains the prescriptions related to the reading of the book of Esther at the *Purim* feast, as well as other literary and liturgical indications.

Mĕnorah. (Derived from *nur,* «light».) Candelabrum with seven arms to be found in the →*Tent of meeting* and, later, in the temple. It is often used as a decorative motif in ancient and modern →*synagogue.*

Mĕturgĕman (translator). Person who translated Hebrew scriptures into →*Aramaean.* The *mĕturgĕman* is a translator of a holy text (the Bible) in a holy place (the →*synagogue)* with the catequetical intention of illustrating and exhorting God's people (the community) in the meaning of the Law's and the Prophets' words (following the liturgical reading cycle), in the same way they were explained and understood in Israel's tradition (in the →*pešat* sense: that is, not merely the literal meaning, but the commonly accepted one, as the *Babylonian* →*Talmud* says: «the sense which even the saduccees agree on» (San 33b).

Mĕzuzah (door jamb). Small box generally metal or wooden, fixed to the door jambs on Jewish houses, containing pieces of parchment on which in 22 lines are written, according to the prescription in Dt 6:6-9 and 11:18-20, the text of Dt 6:4-9 and 11:13-21. On the back of this parchment, rolled from left to right, God's name (Šadday) is written, visible through a small window opened in the box. Those who enter or leave the house usually touch it with their fingers and then kiss them.

180

Midraš (research). Methos of interpreting the Scriptures and also the result produced by this method. It is preferably of a homilitic character. In plural *midrašim* are literary works of biblical commentary, compiled in latter days in vast collections. Modern Jewish authors reserve the name of *midraš* or *midrašim* for Hagadic' texts as oposed to the →*Talmud.*

Minyan (number). The *minyan* indicates *quorum* or the number of ten Jewish males over thirteen required for public Jewish cult. In plural, *minyanim,* is used to refer to a small prayer meeting.

Mishna (repetition). Compendium of oral Jewish law, that is, traditions not included in the Scriptures. The term is almost equivalent to *hălakah.* This teaching, in writing as from the second century, would later form part of the →Talmud. In the →Mishna, the laws are arranges in six chapters: *Zĕra'im* (seeds), *Mo'ed* (fixing of feasts), *Našim* (women), *Nĕzikim* (damage), *Kŏdašim* (holy things) and *Tohŏrot* (purifications). In each of these chapters tractates of different matters are to be found. For example, in the *Mo'ed* chapter are the →*Šabbat* (Sabbath) and *Mĕgillah* [Scroll (of Esther)] tractates. The →*Mishna* is quoted by its tractates and not by chapters.

Mišmar (guard or turn). Division of priests and levites in groups to cover liturgical service in the temple. There were twenty four turns of guard duty.

Ner tamid (eternal light). Light or candle constantly burning in every synagogue to represent continuity of faith.

Paroket. Veil that covers the →*'ăron ha-qodeš.*

Payyĕtan. Name of Byzantian origin given to the synagogue singer or pious Jew who writes religious poems.

Pentateuch. (Derived from Gr. *pente,* five; *teukhos,* scroll: five scrolls.) Name given to the set of the first five books of the Bible (Gn, Ex, Lv, Nm and Dt). They make up the →*Torah* or *Jewish Law.*

Pesaḥ. Passover and unleavened bread feast.

Pešat. Rabbinical interpretation of the Bible according to its straight or literal sense.

Phylacteries. (From Gr. *phylaktêrion,* «object that protects or guards».) Small boxes containing written verses from the Bible that are tied to the forehead or arms. They are called *tĕfillim* in →*Hebrew.* They contain Dt 6:4-9; 11:13-21; Ex 13:1-10 and 11:16. They should be worn during morning prayer, except on the Sabbath and feast days. They are held in place on the head and left arm by leather thongs, which circle the arm seven times and another four times round the same hand and fingers.

Proselyte. Pagan converted to Judaism.

Purim. Feast of lots.

Qeren ha-yobel. The curved horn (Heb. →*qeren*) of a ram (Heb. *yobel*) was used as a musical instrument. This instrument was called *qeren ha-yobel* (ram's horn: Josh 6:5; cf. 1 Par 25:5). Used as a trumpet, *yobel* (which originally meant «ram») also came to mean trumpet. This musical instrument has been reproduced on mosaics that can be seen in →*synagogues* and in Jewish catacombs.

Rabbinical Judaism. Judaism exactly as it is reflected in the →*Mishna*, →*Tosefta'*, →*Talmud* and the →*Midrašim*.
Roš ha-kĕneset. Head of the →*synagogue.*
Roš ha-šanah. New Year's feast.

Šabu'ot. Pentecost or Weeks' feast.
Sebat, Fifteen days of. New Year feast of trees.
Šema' (Hear, [Israel]). First Hebrew word of Dt 6:4-9, the first of the texts that make up the main Jewish prayer. It is recited twice a day, and all adult male Israelites are obliged to do so.
Septuagint, Version of the. The most important Greek version of the Old Testament, known and quoted by the authors of the New Testament. According to Aristeas' letter it is the (only) version written by seventy two scholars in Egypt in times of Ptolomeo. It is quoted using the Roman number LXX.
Siddur. Order for synagogue service. Collection of prayers brought together throughout the centuries and which make up the prayer book for the Jewish congregation.
Simḥat Torah. Feast of the Joy of the Law.
Synagogue (meeting). Centre around which Jewish religious and community life revolves.
Sukkot. Feast of booths, →*tents* or *tabernacles.*

Tallit. Prayer shawl, worn by males at synagogue service.
Talmud (study, teaching). Collection of oral Jewish law put into writing. It is made up of the →*Mishna,* plus its commentary, the →*Gemara,* and other additions called →*baraitot.* Two other important Talmuds existed: the Jerosolimitan one, fourth century, composed in Palestine and also known as Palestinian Talmud and Occidental Talmud, and the Babylonian one, fifth century, composed in the Sura Academy. The Babylonian Talmud supplanted the earlier one in authority and extension. This is the one referred to when using the word Talmud, with no further specification.
Tannaim (repeaters). Jewish teachers from the period in which the →*Mishna* was put down in writing.

Targum (translation). Technical term that refers to the paraphrased translation of biblical texts into →*Aramaean* carried oput by Jews in Palestine and Babylonia for →*synagogue* service.

Tĕfillim. →Phylacteries.

Tent of meeting, of the testimony or tabernacles. Portable sanctuary in the desert, containing the →*ark of the covenant,* considered as Yahve's dwelling in the midst of his people.

Torah (teaching). The Jews' Law; made up of the five books of the →*Pentateuch.*

Tosefta' (supplement). Collection mostly made up of the remains of ancient laws and customs — frequently rejected — combined with tradition later than the →*Mishna.*

Yom Kippur. Feast of Purification.